T0271074

Performance Improvement in Hospitals and Health Systems

Managing Analytics and Quality in Healthcare
2nd Edition

Performance Improvement in Hospitals and Health Systems

Managing Analytics and Quality in Healthcare
2nd Edition

By
James R. Langabeer II, MBA, PhD

CRC Press
Taylor & Francis Group

CRC Press is an imprint of the
Taylor & Francis Group, an **informa** business
A PRODUCTIVITY PRESS BOOK

CRC Press
Taylor & Francis Group
6000 Broken Sound Parkway NW, Suite 300
Boca Raton, FL 33487-2742

© 2018 by Taylor & Francis Group, LLC
CRC Press is an imprint of Taylor & Francis Group, an Informa business

No claim to original U.S. Government works

Printed on acid-free paper

International Standard Book Number-13: 978-1-138-29641-1 (Hardback)
International Standard Book Number-13: 978-1-138-29640-4 (Paperback)
International Standard Book Number-13: 978-1-315-10005-0 (eBook)

Library of Congress Cataloging-in-Publication Data

Names: Langabeer, James R., 1969- editor.
Title: Performance improvement in hospitals and health systems : managing analytics and quality in healthcare / [edited by] James Langabeer II.
Description: 2nd edition. | Boca Raton : Taylor & Francis, 2018. | Revised edition of: Performance improvement in hospitals and health systems / edited by James R. Langabeer II. Chicago, IL : HIMSS, c2009. | "A CRC title, part of the Taylor & Francis imprint, a member of the Taylor & Francis Group, the academic division of T&F Informa plc." | Includes bibliographical references and index.
Identifiers: LCCN 2017044404| ISBN 9781138296404 (paperback : alk. paper) | ISBN 9781138296411 (hardback : alk. paper) | ISBN 9781315100050 (ebook)
Subjects: LCSH: Health services administration. | Medical care--Quality control. | Hospital care--Quality control. | Medical care--Evaluation.
Classification: LCC RA971 .P465 2018 | DDC 362.11--dc23
LC record available at https://lccn.loc.gov/2017044404

Visit the Taylor & Francis Web site at
http://www.taylorandfrancis.com

and the CRC Press Web site at
http://www.crcpress.com

Leadership is the capacity to translate vision into reality.

Dr. Warren Bennis, Management Scholar

Contents

Acknowledgments

The healthcare industry is dynamic, so individuals and organizations must change as well. We grow and improve by reading, by continuous learning, by leading, and by serving our profession. That's why I appreciate the support from the Healthcare Information and Management Systems Society in this second edition. I also appreciate the always rapid responses to my questions from Taylor & Francis senior editor Kristine Mednansky.

Also, as with the first edition, this book would not be possible without the contributed expertise from a few of my colleagues. Their perspectives help provide balance and offer insights and creative perspectives. I appreciate their contributions. Lastly, I wish to acknowledge all the great innovators, researchers, and practitioners who have helped form new theories and pathways for driving quality and change in this industry. There are a lot of health organizations doing some wonderful things, and we are all learning from their successes and failures. I hope that the ideas we present here will spark ideas and actions in those who read this book.

I also really appreciate my wife, Tiffany, for all her love and support.

About the Editor

James Langabeer is professor of biomedical informatics and healthcare management at the University of Texas Health Science Center at Houston. His primary expertise is in strategic and operations management for hospitals and healthcare organizations. Dr. Langabeer has led performance improvement, strategic planning, and business affairs at several large academic medical centers. He was also the founding CEO of a regional health information exchange organization and has consulted for dozens of organizations on quality improvement and strategy.

Jim's research has been funded by multiple national agencies, including the American Heart Association and the Centers for Disease Control and Prevention. Dr. Langabeer has a PhD in management science from the University of Lancaster in England and an MBA from Baylor University, Waco, Texas, and has received advanced training in decision making and negotiation from Harvard Law School, Cambridge, Massachusetts. He is a fellow of the American College of Healthcare Executives, and was designated a fellow of the Healthcare Information and Management Systems Society in 2007.

Jim is the author of multiple books, including *Health Care Operations Management: A Systems Perspective*, 2nd Edition (Jones and Bartlett, 2016). His research has been published in more than 75 journals, including *Health Care Management Review*, *Journal of Healthcare Management*, *Health Care Management Science*, and *Quality Management in Healthcare*.

About the Contributors

Bobbie Kite is the academic director and associate professor of the Healthcare Leadership Program at the University of Denver, University College, Colorado. In addition to working at the University of Denver, she is an adjunct professor at The Ohio State University Wexner Medical Center, Columbus, in the Department of Biomedical Informatics. Dr. Kite's research centers on population health, health data analytics and informatics, and education within these fields. She earned a PhD in healthcare management at the University of Texas School of Public Health, Houston, and completed a postdoctoral fellowship in the clinical and translational research informatics program through the National Library of Medicine at The Ohio State University, Columbus.

Jeffrey R. Helton is an associate professor of healthcare management at Metropolitan State University of Denver, Colorado, teaching health economics, healthcare finance, and health informatics. He is a Certified Management Accountant, a Certified Fraud Examiner, and a fellow of the Healthcare Financial Management Association. He has worked as chief financial officer in the industry, bringing 28 years of experience leading the finance function for hospitals, health plans, and integrated health systems across the United States. Jeff earned a PhD in healthcare management at the University of Texas School of Public Health, Houston; a master of health administration from the University of Alabama at Birmingham; and a BBA from Eastern Kentucky University, Richmond. Dr. Helton is also a coauthor of the textbook *Health Care Operations Management: A Systems Perspective* (Jones and Bartlett, 2016).

Kim Brant-Lucich is the information services (IS) site director for Little Company of Mary Medical Center in Southbay, California, Providence Health and Services. She is responsible for overseeing hospital IS operations, including infrastructure, desktop support, and strategic alignment of business and information technology (IT) initiatives. Prior to joining Providence, Kim served in a variety of executive IS and process redesign roles for Zynx Health and St. Joseph Health in Orange, California. In her prior roles, she developed a comprehensive, web-enabled, reusable methodology for process redesign and change management for system implementation projects. She also worked with IT and business executives to develop their IT strategic road maps and value propositions for IT initiatives. In addition to her current responsibilities, Kim is an adjunct faculty and lecturer of Advanced Healthcare Information Technology at Cal State University, Long Beach. Kim is past national chair of the Healthcare Information and Management Systems Society (HIMSS) Management Engineering-Performance Improvement Community and has also served on the national HIMSS health information exchange committee. Kim has an MBA from the University of Southern California, Los Angeles, and a bachelor of arts degree from the University of California at Davis. She holds a Project Management Professional (PMP) certification and is a volunteer instructor for the Project Management Institute's PMP prep course.

Osama Mikhail currently serves as senior vice president of strategic planning at the University of Texas Health Science Center, Houston. He is also a professor of management and policy sciences at the University of Texas, School of Public Health. At the school, Dr. Mikhail teaches courses in healthcare finance, planning, and management, and advises students in both the master and doctoral programs. Previously, Dr. Mikhail was an executive for multiple health systems. At St. Luke's Episcopal Health System in Houston, he served as chief planning and chief strategic officer. Dr. Mikhail received a BS in math and physics from the American University of Beirut in Lebanon; an MBA in finance from the University of Pennsylvania's Wharton School, Philadelphia; and an MS in industrial administration and a PhD in systems sciences from the Graduate School of Industrial Administration at Carnegie Mellon University in Pittsburgh, Pennsylvania. Dr. Mikhail is a coauthor of *Integrating Quality and Strategy in Health Care Organizations* (Jones and Bartlett, 2012).

Rigoberto (Rigo) Delgado is a health economist and associate professor of healthcare management and economics at the University of Texas at El Paso. Dr. Delgado also holds a joint appointment at the University of

Texas School of Public Health, Houston. He has worked as an economist, management consultant, and executive for several organizations. His primary expertise is in cost-effectiveness methods, health services research, healthcare finance, and population health analytics. Rigoberto has a PhD in health economics and management from the University of Texas School of Public Health and an MBA from the University of California at Berkeley. Dr. Delgado is fluent in Spanish and has worked in the United States, Latin America, Middle East, and England. Rigo also serves on several boards of charity health clinics in Texas. In 2005, the U.S. secretary of agriculture appointed Rigoberto to serve on the National Organic Standards Board, and he served as the chair of the board in 2008.

Tiffany Champagne-Langabeer is an assistant professor at the University of Texas Health Science Center, School of Biomedical Informatics, Houston. Dr. Champagne-Langabeer's expertise is in health information exchange, health policy, and technology. She was the vice president of a large regional health information exchange, where she was one of the initial founding members of the management team. She is a registered dietitian and has an undergraduate degree in nutrition from the University of Texas; an MBA from the University of St. Thomas, Saint Paul, Minnesota; and a PhD in health management and policy from the University of Texas School of Public Health, Houston. Tiffany's research has been published in multiple academic journals, including the *Journal of the American Heart Association* and *Quality Management in Healthcare*.

Introduction

Intelligence is the ability to adapt to change.

Dr. Stephen Hawking
Theoretical Physicist

In the few years since the first edition was published, much has changed in the world. Presidential politics have continued to make healthcare financing and delivery a topic of great debate. Lack of certainty around the health insurance marketplace and other provisions of the Affordable Care Act have created some ambiguity and turmoil. Reimbursement policies from payers are also constantly shifting. Organizations have responded in many ways. We have seen much greater emphasis on data analytics to identify gaps and drive down costs in the system. There is much more use of telehealth, remote monitoring, ambulatory care, and other alternative delivery mechanisms. There is also a heightened focus on the health of "populations" and not just "individuals." This has led to a growth in population health management. Stimulating technology investments (through electronic health records and health information exchanges) have received less attention and funding in the past few years, however.

To keep up with these changes, there needs to be significantly greater emphasis on analyses and analytics, everything from predictive modeling of admissions, to data mining of "profitable" payers and patients, to linear modeling of readmissions. Performance and quality improvement professionals will continue to incorporate data and analytics into their tool kits. In this edition, we address these topics covering population health, quality management, and business analytics.

This second edition seeks to address many of the challenges that health systems are having with regards to using technology and analyses to drive changes in results. We have significantly expanded on the coverage of all these topics. The themes of this book are summarized in Figure 0.1.

For nearly two decades, I have been researching and practicing health-care management. In my view, management is essentially about guiding others to achieve better results, but this is not the exclusive domain of a manager—it is an inherent component of every individual's job description within an organization, from the bottom to the top. We get better when clinical units strive for lower infection rates, when housekeepers aim to turn beds and rooms faster, and when patients have less idle time in a waiting room. This book is written for those of you who take your role seriously and wish to raise the level of performance in your own organization.

In this second edition, we commonly use the terms *performance improvement* and *quality management* synonymously. There are technical distinctions between them, as we will describe in the first chapter, but they essentially refer to the same set of practices and concepts. These concepts need to be understood by managers and executives, but they will be used daily by some of you—those of you who struggle daily to combat the status quo, using a combination of methods to change systems and processes. Some organizations call these people industrial or management engineers, but most go by many other names—quality coordinator, operations analyst, process consultant, project manager, black belt, Six Sigma consultant, business process analyst, process improvement analyst, management analyst, and quality manager are some of the more common titles. Small differences aside, these are key positions that help to lead change and improve performance. You will notice that we use these terms interchangeably in this book. But more importantly, every administrator and executive that devotes

Figure 0.1   Trends in healthcare.

the majority of his or her time to making things better, not just maintaining the status quo, is really a performance improvement professional.

Since the field of quality management and performance improvement is expanding rapidly, it is difficult (or impossible) to find any one expert in the area who understands the theory and practice of all the methods used by leading health systems. So, I turned to several colleagues and recognized experts in this area for help. In this book, we have assembled multiple individuals who have extensive practical and scholarly knowledge around these topics. These experts share their methods, results, and best practices. All of them have spent multiple years in a hospital or health organization leading change, as well as in providing scholarly research in an academic setting. Each of these authors brings his or her own unique experience and perspective to these topics, and the book is much more comprehensive as a result. I asked the authors to write on the topics they are most interested in or passionate about.

This book should be useful in classrooms, but it is not intended to be theoretical in nature. I hope it is applied, practical, and actionable. Healthcare organizations have a long way to go to master their process workflows, information and management systems, and overall performance. It is my expectation that this book will significantly advance this discussion by providing valuable insights into what practitioners are doing to control and improve their environments.

This book is written for all those in health systems who are charged with not just maintaining the status quo, but delivering results. Executives, administrators, managers, analysts, physicians, nurses, and pharmacists all will benefit from better understanding process and performance improvement. I think this is a timely and relevant book, as hospitals, clinics, and systems begin or continue their improvement journey. I hope the chapters in this book contribute to that outcome.

QUALITY AND PERFORMANCE IN HEALTH

In the first two chapters, we explore the theories and concepts underlying performance improvement. Chapter 1 provides a very in-depth discussion of quality and quality management. Quality pioneers and theories are described, along with the various perspectives on quality in healthcare. Chapter 2 describes the link between strategy and operational effectiveness, and provides a framework for performance management. It is important to note that the term *performance* means different things to different people, depending on your perspective and the setting. In the retail industry, a customer might consider performance to be the quality of the product she is buying, while the retail executives might view it as return on assets or same-store year-over-year sales growth. In healthcare, performance is a broad and complicated topic. A provider might look at safety or process of care measures, while administrators and the board of trustees might define performance in financial terms. Analysts should know that quality and performance management is multidimensional, and is defined by clinical, quality, financial, and strategic dimensions. Before we try to improve, we need to know which area we are focusing on.

Chapter 1

Quality and Quality Management

James Langabeer

Contents

An organization's ability to learn, and translate that learning into action rapidly, is the ultimate competitive advantage.

Jack Welch
Former CEO of General Electric

Introduction

Quality is defined both internally (did we meet specifications?) and externally (did our customers and patients receive the value they expected?). Quality management philosophy guides all performance improvement for an organization. Performance improvement is essentially about changing results for an organization, whether it is a clinic, hospital, surgical center, health department, insurance company, or healthcare delivery system. Implied in this are changes to both the inputs and the process that produce those outcomes. There is generally ambiguity about definitions and differences between process improvement, performance improvement, and quality improvement, and many other terms. In this chapter, we review the theories and concepts underlying quality management and performance improvement.

Quality

Remember, just a few years back, when the American car industry was heading toward disaster? Quality—in the eyes of the consumers who purchased and drove these vehicles—was gauged to be extremely low and sales declined to such a point that countries such as Japan and Germany were thought to be the only places to find quality. Some U.S. carmakers had even declared bankruptcy. The competitiveness of American car manufacturers was limited. But then the American car industry rebounded and now tops many of the consumer quality ratings for different car types. At the same time, other countries, such as South Korea, have also emerged as leaders. What happened? Changes in design, manufacturing, and service. In short, process and quality improvement allowed companies to focus on consumer needs.

Similarly, the healthcare industry is trying to rebound from its own crisis. The landmark report by the National Academy of Medicine (formerly the Institute of Medicine), called *To Err Is Human*, helped to create a national awareness of the significant quality and safety issue surrounding health (Kohn et al., 2000). The report estimated that between 44,000 and 98,000 people die every year from preventable accidents and errors in hospitals. The combined costs of these deaths and other quality issues alone could amount to up to $29 billion each year.

We start with a basic definition for quality. *Quality* is a perception of the level of value a customer places on an organization's outputs, and the degree to which these meet established specifications and benchmarks. Everything an organization does impacts quality, from the type of furniture to the recruitment of employees. Quality is reflected at both the institutional level (e.g., overall number of medical errors) and the process or departmental level (e.g., aspirins administered to cardiac patients).

Even the use of basic information technology (IT), such as the *electronic health record* (EHR), creates potential quality concerns. An EHR is a comprehensive longitudinal electronic record that stores patient health data in a hospital or clinic, including patient demographics, prior medical history, interventions performed, laboratory and test results, and medications (Healthcare Information and Systems Society, 2017).

Sittig and Singh (2012) point out that EHR information systems have a significant impact on quality, including miscommunication between providers; system downtime and access issues that impact patients; "alert fatigue," where providers override system messages; and many other quality concerns resulting from failure to adopt and implement new systems properly.

Aside from clinical quality and outcomes, there are issues with regard to the quality of business and administrative processes. There is an extremely high amount of inefficiency and administrative waste, in everything from revenue cycle to supply chain management. Prominent researchers have claimed that nearly $1 trillion in wasteful spending occurs because of administrative complexity, process failures, fraud and abuse, overtreatment, and overspending, among others (Sahni et al., 2015; Berwick and Hackbarth, 2012).

Quality costs can be high. *Cost of quality* represents the sum of all costs associated with providing inferior, error-prone, or poor-quality services. Some of these are the avoidable costs of failure, defects, and errors (e.g., surgery on the wrong body part or an avoidable hospital readmission). Other costs are necessary, such as the cost of preventing errors (e.g., checklists and protocols). Then there are the opportunity costs of what your organization could have done with the resources that went into poor quality and rework. Cost of quality is the sum of all costs to avoid, prevent, and provide inferior services.

Cleary, quality is a major concern. Improving quality and performance needs to be taken seriously. The term *quality* conjures up a lot of different definitions. Despite lots of attention, there is still ambiguity surrounding the precise meaning of quality (Reeves and Bednar, 1994). Quality can be defined by multiple dimensions, including the following:

- *Customer*: Customers pay bills, so this definition suggests meeting (or exceeding) the customer's expectations. Of course, in healthcare, the term *customer* is also confusing, since we have a separation between the consumer of the service and the payer in many respects. Regardless, many marketing and management scholars over the years have thought that organizations should deliver what the customer wants and needs, and that if they meet those expectations, then the products will sell and the company will grow (Buzzell and Gale, 1987; Deming, 1986). This is one of the most important definitions for quality in healthcare.
- *Value*: Quality is often seen as being equal to the value produced in terms of total outcomes in relationship to their costs. Dr. Michael Porter, a leading scholar from the Harvard Business School, suggests that this definition is the most applicable to healthcare (Porter, 2010). It makes sense, because everything we do to improve quality should be considered relative to its cost. If we add 10 patient rooms to reduce wait times, is that change in service level offset by higher costs that cannot be recovered? *Value* in healthcare is an expression of the relationship between outcomes produced by an organization and costs over time.
- *Fitness for use*: The term *fitness for use* was created by Joseph Juran to indicate that the product or service should do what it is intended to do. Users (customers) should be able to count on it to do what it is supposed to do (Juran, 1992). In healthcare, this would suggest that customers intend for our physicians' diagnoses and treatments to be correct, and to help heal us. Waiting rooms should be comfortable enough, technology should support the process, and staff should be trained appropriately. All these suggest fitness for use.
- *Conformance*: Quality is often viewed in terms of how well it meets or conforms to the specifications or requirements for the product or service (Crosby, 1979). This definition cares less about how the customer views it, and more about whether it is delivered as designed. This definition seems to work well in some areas, such as manufacturing. In terms of healthcare, it isn't widely applied.
- *Excellence*: Quality has been defined as the pursuit of the highest standards and results, and not settling for average or typical outcomes (Peters and Waterman, 1984). We see this when we look at specific institutions that seem be strive for excellence daily. Certain health

systems are continually innovating and excelling. But, this definition cannot be for everybody, since excellence does have a cost. Or can it be?

So, is quality conformance to a specification? Excellence? Meeting or exceeding a customer's expectations? Achieving value? It's these things, or maybe a mix of them, depending on your own organization's strategy and beliefs. How do you currently perceive your organization's quality relative to that of others? Analysts should always first examine how leadership in their organization enables and operationalizes quality. What is being discussed at organizational staff meetings? What are the primary drivers of concern?

Quality can be defined in different ways, making performance improvement more difficult. It is essential to understand how your organization defines and implements quality into its strategy to focus on improvements.

Delivery organizations should make sure they include aspects of patient satisfaction, health, and safety outcomes relative to costs (value), and adherence to the latest clinical evidence. *Evidence* is empirical data, or proof, supporting a decision or position. Health and safety outcomes in this case should be both prevention (e.g., preventable readmissions or acquired infections) and clinical process of care (compliance with guideline-based aspirin or medication interventions). It is vital that your organization ensures that its agrees on how it wishes to define quality, and aligns that with internal staff and stakeholders. To change quality, there must be alignment in the organization. A quality management approach should drive your performance improvement efforts.

Quality Management

Quality management is a management philosophy focused on systematically improving performance and processes (Deming, 1986; Dean and Bowen, 1994). Quality management is necessary to guide business and clinical performance improvement, and to achieve organizational competitiveness. *Competitiveness* is the ability of an organization to provide goods and services that are superior to those of rivals, and produce value for customers and long-term sustainability. If done correctly, this involves assumptions and principles that flow through the organization, resulting in changes to culture and beliefs in the leadership and employees. *Culture* refers to the core values and beliefs shared by all employees and management in an organization. A commitment to quality helps organizations continuously strive for better results over time. It suggests a relentless pursuit of positive change in outcomes, efficiency, and overall outcomes.

Improving quality is necessary to achieve better results, and a high-quality strategy can produce significant gains in strategic measures, such as market share, profitability, and overall competitiveness (Buzzell and Gale, 1987). It can also significantly reduce medical and medication errors, improve patient safety, and drive other meaningful improvements in clinical care. In this era of heightened competition, the edge gained from better quality is vital.

A quality management approach embeds many different foci, and we discuss these throughout the book. But, at a minimum, the formula driving quality management includes organizational strategy, culture and teamwork, customer focus, and methods (for defining, analyzing, measuring, and improving). Figure 1.1 summarizes the quality management formula.

A strategy should commit the organization to achieving superior quality and improving perceived quality by customers (patients). *Strategy* sets the organizational direction and provides details on how the vision will be enabled. We focus more on this in Chapter 2 "Strategy and Performance Management". Strategy requires solid leadership, focused on doing things right and doing the right things. Leaders in high-quality health organizations provide direction that enables employees to make the right decisions, fixated on customers, outcomes, costs, and value. Strategy and leadership are interconnected.

In addition, successful hospitals and health systems should adopt a long-term horizon and organizational culture that rewards improvements, and continuously changes through systemic process modeling that weeds out waste and improves outcomes. Culture is difficult to change, especially in more mature and established organizations, but recognition of efforts and rewards for process changes helps to stimulate a quality culture. Teamwork is an important aspect of culture. Teamwork fosters internal partnerships

Figure 1.1   Quality management formula.

and collaboration between different people and departments to achieve results.

Importantly, there must be a focus on customers, both external and internal. Customer focus helps to improve transparency and provide services that customers really want and need. The culture needs to support the emphasis on customers, and not staff or physicians.

Finally, organizations need to adopt a methodology for improvement and the use of tools and techniques. Throughout this book, we describe several of them, but most basic methods require an approach to defining and structuring a problem, measuring current performance, setting goals, making process changes, and continuously improving and refining. Methodologies such as Six Sigma, Lean, or plan–do–check–act (PDCA) are similar in many respects, but different in others. These are the focus of Chapter 3. Regardless of the chosen methodology, analysts should make use of tools and techniques, such as forecasting, predictive modeling, and simulation.

Core Components of Quality Management

There are many different beliefs and principles of quality management that have been identified over time by different researchers, including Shewhart, Deming, Juran, and Crosby. We describe a few of the contributions from the early leaders in the field.

Dr. Walter Shewhart (an engineer and physicist) was the first researcher to describe the need for and methods used in quality control. Shewhart published landmark texts on this field in the early 1930s, influencing the next three quality gurus after him, who began in the 1950s. Shewhart is best known as the founder of the PDCA cycle, which is in extensive use today as the dominant methodology in healthcare organizations.

Dr. W. Edwards Deming (an engineer and statistician) helped to create a philosophy of management that uses statistical analysis to reduce variation or variability in processes and outcomes. *Variability* refers to the relative degree of dispersion of data points, especially as they differ from the norm. Deming created control charts and other tools that continue in use today. He strongly believed that management needs to embrace a culture focused on continuous improvement for any change to be successful. This included a focus on long-term profits, constancy of organizational purpose, and stability in the management among others, which he defined in his "fourteen points" and "seven deadly diseases" (Deming, 2000).

Dr. Joseph Juran (an engineer and consultant) also believed that quality improvement should be integrated into management theory. He was the first to apply the Pareto principle to quality. The Pareto principle states that 80% of a problem can be attributed to 20% of the cause. He advocated the use of a *Pareto chart*, which is a combination bar–line graph depicting individual and cumulative frequency represented in descending order. The frequency or outcome is shown on the Y axis, and the reasons or causes for that are shown on the X axis. He also developed the three phases of quality management (planning, control, and improvement), which we will describe further in the next section. These phases are critical to the belief that quality improvements lead to long-term performance improvements (Juran, 1989).

Philip B. Crosby (a quality manager) was the first to state that "zero defects," or error-free production, should be the norm, and not the exception. *Zero defect* is a philosophy that expects managers to prevent errors before they begin, which reduces total costs by doing things right the first time (Crosby, 1979). As stated in his book, Crosby believed that "quality is free," implying that prevention of errors will pay for itself in the long-run.

Of course, there are others who made significant contributions. Dr. Genichi Taguchi emphasized designing in quality the first time. Dr. Kaoru Ishikawa created the concept of a cause-and-effect diagram (now called "fishbone" diagrams). There are many others from the fields of quality, statistics, and management that all had influences on quality and performance improvement. Although all had unique contributions, they seemingly agree in a few common areas. Table 1.1 summarizes the key principles of quality.

Table 1.1 Quality Principles

■ Quality can only be achieved by continuous measurement and focus.
■ Decision making should be driven by data.
■ Performance gains will be realized when the organization is committed to them.
■ The people who do the work are best positioned to improve on it.
■ Teamwork is essential.
■ A systems orientation ensures that organizations don't optimize one process that negatively impacts the whole.

Planning, Improvement, and Control

Juran described three primary phases in improving performance and quality: planning, improvement, and control. Together, these activities raise the performance levels for organizations. Later, we will discuss how these are integrated in the common performance improvement methodologies, such as PDCA or Six Sigma. Figure 1.2 shows the improvement cycle.

Planning for quality and performance involves addressing the issue of how your organization defines quality. Fundamentally, this entails defining whether that means "patient satisfaction" or "conformance to requirements" or "value." Once it is understood, and leadership shares this and creates a common culture around it, then planning should address how to ensure that this is met. The planning process should adopt specific methodologies for how performance will be improved, and embrace the tools and techniques that will be used across the institution. These tools might include flowcharting, benchmarking, statistical sampling, customer satisfaction surveys, and many others that will be discussed in subsequent chapters.

Improvement includes the activities necessary to ensure that your organization is following the standards and requirements that were established in the planning phase. Improvement involves making changes to processes that work toward desired goals. There are several different methods and analytics we use to improve processes.

Control processes ensure that we meet quality standards, and tend to be the primary focus of continuous improvement. *Statistical process control* (SPC) is the term used for applying statistics to monitor and control

Figure 1.2 Improvement cycle.

the behavior of a process. Routine audits of performance are typically conducted, as well as process analysis using flowcharts, cause-and-effect diagrams, histograms, and other visualizations to bring processes to desired levels.

Need for Healthcare Improvement

As we approach the year 2020, there is a greater need for change and improvement than ever before, especially in healthcare. The term *Kaizen* is the Japanese word for continuous improvement. Kaizen should be the standard practice in healthcare. Medical costs continue to grow at rates nearly triple those of other industries, despite technology and other efforts to curb their growth. Health outcomes, quality, and cost-effectiveness of healthcare processes have become center stage for every hospital or healthcare system. U.S. healthcare expenditures in 2009 were just $2 trillion annually (four times the national defense budget, or about $7,500 per person). In 2020, the Centers for Medicare and Medicaid Services project it to be around $4.2 trillion, or $12,500 per capita (CMS, 2017). That rate of growth in costs over a decade is phenomenal—and unsustainable.

A big part of this expense is purely waste—waste in terms of duplication of effort, overutilization of resources, and inefficient administration and clinical processes. While federal government and macrolevel policy change might bring change in the long term, in the near-term change must come from within organizations. Who do these organizations—the hospitals, clinics, and systems—look to for promoting change internally? Quality and performance improvement professionals.

At the same time, quality of care is under close examination. Organizations can do much better in terms of reducing medical and medication errors. That is the role of administrators, analysts, and other professionals—to enhance the performance and quality of clinical and administrative processes. As process and system experts, these professionals must begin to play a broader role in redefining healthcare in the United States, and bringing cost-effective healthcare to our hospitals and health systems.

So, you might ask, what is the role and purpose of a quality improvement manager or management engineer, and why should healthcare organizations invest in them? Everyone intuitively understands why clinics and hospitals need physicians and nurses, and most quickly agree that as technology becomes more integrated and essential to patient care, IT professionals are necessary, but only a small minority fully understand and appreciate the full potential of professionals dedicated to improving the performance of management systems, workflow, and outcomes. Yet, the value and contribution of the professionals that dedicate their efforts to performance and process improvement daily are substantial.

Industrial engineering techniques have been applied to healthcare since the early 1900s. While industrial engineers such as Frank and Lillian Gilbreth focused on process efficiency, others, such as Frederick Taylor, worked on improving productivity using time and motion studies. Together, these early pioneers showed surgeons and providers that the healthcare industry could benefit from process improvement much the same as manufacturing industries (Heineke and Davis, 2007). This is evident in efforts to redesign the clinician's workflow to increase outputs in the operating room, for example. The field was significantly advanced by Harold Smalley, one of the founding fathers of the Healthcare Management Systems Society—which later became the Healthcare Information and Management Systems Society. Since this time, we have seen growth in the number of organizations, journals, and training opportunities in the "science of improvement," but it is still insufficient. We need greater penetration of employees focused on attacking the obstacles and roadblocks facing healthcare, and using a combination of engineering and organizational development techniques.

Performance Improvement

Quality management (QM) professionals focus on improving quality and performance. *Performance improvement* is an approach that analyzes, measures, and changes business and clinical processes to improve outcomes. Performance improvement involves establishing better management systems. *Management systems* are the framework of all processes, policies, procedures, standards, and other documentation that defines how an organization should behave in order to achieve its purpose. Management systems outline the work environment that must be conducted to execute daily operations. *Performance* reflects the inputs, process, and outcomes (results) for specific areas. Performance improvement analysts apply engineering, statistical, and analytical techniques to understand the behavior or processes and then work with teams to create recommendations for process change.

While historically in healthcare quality and PI professionals were trained as engineers, they became known as management engineers. *Management engineering* in the healthcare arena can be defined as the application of engineering principles to healthcare processes. It focuses on designing optimal management and information systems and processes, using tools from engineering, mathematics, and social sciences.

Most commonly, performance improvement approaches start with analysis of the behavior of processes using a framework that ensures that decisions are analytical and data driven. We tend to express variables and activities in quantitative terms, using actual data obtained from information systems or calculated from observations. This mapping of process behavior and modeling in statistical ways is essential to identify areas for improvement, and then measure the effects of change.

This often resembles a mathematical or engineering approach, where science is applied to decisions. This approach supports data-driven management. *Data-driven management* is the use of proven and established organizational practices to improve decisions and results (Langabeer and Helton, 2016; Walshe and Rundall, 2001). Data-driven management suggests that data drives decisions, not just assumptions and intuitions. This requires a systems orientation. *Systems orientation* understands that all activities and processes are interconnected, and that change in one produces change elsewhere. This is not just referring to "information" systems, but management and organizational systems, and the activities for the healthcare ecosystem. A policy for evaluating employees, for example, is a management system. So too are procedures for handling patient complaints.

Performance improvement incorporates cost-effectiveness as well, by understanding not just results, but also the relationship between incremental value produced from a process and its associated costs. As described earlier, value in healthcare is an expression of the relationship between outcomes produced by an organization and costs over time. Since most gains in performance come only through additional expenses (such as investing in new technology or equipment), quality analysts can help play a valuable role in identifying useful practices that have high cost-effectiveness, thereby ensuring that resources are applied optimally.

There are a number of areas to focus on, and a number of different job titles and roles in organizations that help in performance improvement. These roles and areas of focus are shown in Figure 1.3.

While quality and performance professionals in the past can best be classified as "tacticians" or "technicians," today's analysts are agents of

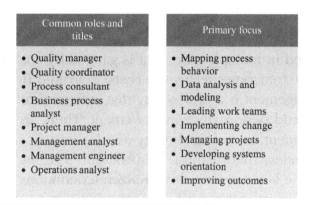

Common roles and titles	Primary focus
• Quality manager • Quality coordinator • Process consultant • Business process analyst • Project manager • Management analyst • Management engineer • Operations analyst	• Mapping process behavior • Data analysis and modeling • Leading work teams • Implementing change • Managing projects • Developing systems orientation • Improving outcomes

Figure 1.3   Roles and focus in performance improvement.

change. They are internal consultants that help executives better manage projects; they are leaders of key IT and capital projects; they use collaboration and facilitation skills to guide team efforts; and they understand performance drivers and technology better than anyone in the organization to help make changes stick. Performance improvement has become an issue for the boardroom, and now is the time for engineers and analysts to expand their tool kit and take a visible leadership role in organizational change.

The breadth and scope of performance improvement and quality management professionals are growing. Analysts and quality coordinators can get involved in a variety of different activities and projects. Examples of these are shown in Table 1.2.

Table 1.2   Types of Quality and Performance Improvement Activities

Implementation of systems and technology	New facility construction projects
Development of business plans	Process workflow redesign
Performance benchmarking	Productivity and staffing management
Supply chain reengineering	Simulation modeling of clinics and units
Cataloging and deploying evidence to improve medical quality	Data mining for decision making

Summary

Quality is measured in multiple ways, but is gauged by customers' perceptions and the value (outcomes relative to costs) delivered by the organization. Quality management is a philosophy that systematically improves long-term quality and performance improvement. There are multiple pillars of quality management, including strategy and leadership, measurement and improvement activities, culture and teamwork, and a strong commitment to the customer. Three key activities drive Kaizen (continuous improvement): planning, improvement, and control. Performance improvement is those efforts geared to delivering improved results and outcomes, with full awareness of the impact on overall costs and resource utilization.

Key Terms

Competitiveness, cost of quality, culture, electronic health record, evidence, data-driven management, Kaizen, management engineering, management systems, Pareto chart, performance, performance improvement, statistical process control, strategy, systems orientation, quality, quality management, value, variability, zero defects

Discussion Questions

1. How competitive do you think most hospitals are today?
2. What does quality mean to you? To your organization?
3. As a healthcare consumer, do you believe you can objectively find quality measures on your physicians and hospitals? Why or why not?
4. If you were the CEO, what would you do differently to ensure higher quality?
5. Will the concept of zero defects ever be a reality in healthcare?

References

Berwick D and Hackbarth A (2012). Eliminating waste in US health care. *Journal of the American Medical Association (JAMA)*, 307(14), 1513–1516.
Buzzell R and Gale B (1987). *The Profit Impact of Marketing Strategy: Linking Strategy to Performance*. New York: The Free Press.

CMS (Centers for Medicare and Medicaid Services) (2017). National health expenditures, 2016–2025 forecast summary. Available at www.cms.gov.

Crosby P (1979). *Quality Is Free: The Art of Making Quality Certain.* New York: New American Library.

Dean J and Bowen D (1994). Managing theory and total quality: Improving research and practice through theory development. *Academy of Management Review,* 19(3), 392–418.

Deming WE (1986). *Quality, Productivity, and Competitive Position.* Cambridge: Massachusetts Institute of Technology Center for Advanced Engineering Study.

Deming WE (2000). *Out of the Crisis.* Cambridge, MA: MIT Press.

Heineke J and Davis M (2007). The emergence of service operations management as an academic discipline. *Journal of Operations Management,* 25(2), 364–374.

Juran JM (1989). *Juran on Leadership for Quality.* New York: Free Press.

Juran JM (1992). *Juran on Quality by Design: The New Steps for Planning Quality into Goods and Services.* New York: Free Press.

Langabeer J and Helton J (2016). *Health Care Operations Management: A Systems Perspective.* Boston, MA. Jones and Bartlett Publishers.

Kohn LT, Corrigan JM, and Donaldson MS, eds. (2000). *To Err Is Human: Building a Safer Health System.* Washington, DC: National Academies Press.

Peters T and Waterman R (1984). *In Search of Excellence: Lessons from America's Best-Run Companies.* New York: Grand Central Publishing.

Porter M (2010). What is value in health care? *New England Journal of Medicine,* 363, 2477–2481.

Reeves C and Bednar D (1994). Defining quality: Alternatives and implications. *Academy of Management Review,* 19(3), 419–445.

Sahni N, Chigurupati A, Kocher B, and Cutler D (2015). How the U.S. can reduce healthcare spending by $1 trillion. *Harvard Business Review,* October 13, 2015, pp. 1–9.

Sittig D and Singh H (2012). Electronic health records and national patient-safety goals. *New England Journal of Medicine,* 367, 1854–1860.

Walshe K and Rundall TG (2001). Evidence-based management: From theory to practice in health care. *Milbank Quarterly,* 79, 429–457.

Chapter 2

Strategy and Performance Management

James Langabeer and Osama Mikhail

Contents

> The thing is, continuity of strategic direction and continuous improvement in how you do things are absolutely consistent with each other. In fact, they're mutually reinforcing.
>
> **Dr. Michael Porter**
>
> *Strategy Scholar*

Introduction

The concept of improving performance requires that organizations understand their current performance, and then develop a vision about future performance levels. In many respects, this requires that managers approach each project as a component of the strategic planning process. Strategy and operations are mutually reinforcing. Most importantly, performance improvement requires knowledge about strategy, different dimensions of performance, and how to establish performance targets. Performance management is key to long-term change. All this is described in this chapter.

Performance Management

Organizations continuously seek to improve their performance. *Performance management* refers to the process by which organizations align their resources, systems, and employees to strategies and objectives. Nonprofit, governmental, and healthcare organizations are not exempt from this process of managing toward strategic goals. Hospitals and health systems obviously exist for many reasons, such as to heal the sick, to improve the health of the community, and to research new treatments. The core services provided within health organizations typically include observation, diagnosis, treatment, and rehabilitation. Notice that these all revolve around patients and the public's health—which can be measured clinically or medically. Quality measures and medical outcomes could be used to assess if the health system did a reasonable job in these areas. Key questions to ask are

■ Did the patient expire or live?
■ Did the patient make a full recovery?
■ Did other complications arise during the patient's stay?

These types of questions have led the industry to historically measure things in terms of two key metrics: mortality and morbidity. *Mortality* is a measure of the rate of incidence for deaths, while *morbidity* is a measure of the rate of illness. These are good macrolevel indicators that reflect long-term efforts, but they don't tell an organization much. These measures are too broad to really allow physicians and administrators to concentrate efforts on clinical improvements.

So, many other more intermediate clinical outcomes and indicators that are linked to the broad metrics are now being used to better measure performance. Frequency of medical errors and incorrect filling of pharmaceutical prescriptions are two commonly utilized metrics. There are many to choose from, as you will see.

Yet healthcare involves more than clinical outcomes. All organizations are normally expected to be a "going concern," and therefore are expected to continue operations for the long term. This suggests survival, and to survive in the long term, organizations must have control over financial results—such as cash flows, margins, debt, and working capital. *Key performance indicators* (KPIs) are quantitative measures of performance used to evaluate the success that an organization has in meeting established objectives. There are organizational, strategic, and financial metrics. Financial KPIs for healthcare are shown in Table 2.1, and we will discuss these in much more detail in Chapter 8 "Analytics in Healthcare Organizations".

Financial results, though, are dictated by operations and strategy. Operationally, factors such as the number of personnel, productivity, investment of information technology, space, and facilities layout are all key to driving operational results (Langabeer and Helton, 2016). Strategically, organizations must focus on market share, growth rates, branding, and other key outcomes. Figure 2.1 shows how performance measures reflect long-term success in hospitals and health systems.

Table 2.1 Key Financial Metrics

Financial Category	Key Performance Indicator
Profitability	• Operating margin • Profit margin • Earnings before interest, taxes, depreciation, amortization, and rent (EBITDA) • Return on assets • Return on equity
Debt management	• Debt–equity ratio • Debt per bed (or discharge, adjusted patient day)
Efficiency	• Average payment period • Asset turnover • Inventory conversion ratio
Capital	• Net present value • Internal rate of return • Payback period

So, performance has multiple dimensions, all of which are important in different ways and times. Since performance improvement professionals are typically focused on "projects," the first task is to understand which aspect of performance to focus our efforts on. To do this, we need a framework for comprehensively understanding performance in healthcare.

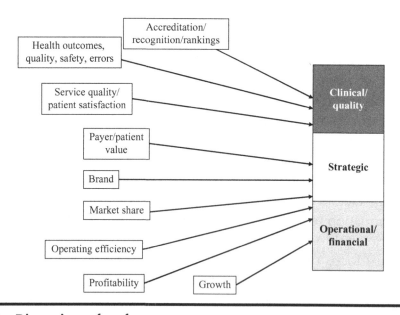

Figure 2.1 Dimensions of performance.

Healthcare Strategy and Performance for Nonprofits

The performance of healthcare organizations is typically measured by the extent to which it achieved or contributed toward the mission and vision of the organization. Since most health systems and hospitals are not for profit, the mission is often stated in less financial terms and is more about serving the community, improving health outcomes, and increasing service and clinical quality.

Many not-for-profit organizations base their purpose and existence on a stated mission, usually defined in terms of meeting specific community needs. This makes it difficult to hold them accountable for performance related to mission because the specific metrics related to how well the mission is being fulfilled are often neglected or difficult to measure. The performance measures that organizations are generally held to are often "means" objectives, as opposed to the mission "ends." For example, mission often calls the organization to provide health services that improve community health status and enhance quality of life; however, typical performance measures for which management is held accountable are generally metrics such as profitability, return on investment, market share, and quality of care or service. Translating these to improvements in health status and quality of life might not be impossible, but certainly challenging. So, the fundamental question is, how do society, boards, and others hold organizations accountable for fulfilling their missions? How do we back into an assessment or judgment on how well management is doing with respect to mission and not just simply the means measures of performance. To that end, we should move toward more direct ways of measuring "mission performance" so that we can evaluate organizations and management in terms of how well they're doing with respect to their core purpose, that is, the organization's mission. This will allow us to hold management and governance "accountable" for what they profess to be their purpose or mission. This is termed *mission accountability* (Langabeer, 2009; Sadhegi et al., 2012).

With regards to mission accountability, there are three dimensions that need measured:

1. How *much* an organization does toward its stated mission (measures of quantity)
2. How *well* an organization does it (one view of quality)
3. How efficient the organization is at doing things (cost-effectiveness)

If we blend these three dimensions together (quantity, quality, and cost-effectiveness), we have a very good understanding of what healthcare organizations must do to survive and thrive today. Strategic performance for most healthcare organizations is therefore the sum of both mission performance and organizational performance, as shown below.

Performance Framework

In publicly traded industrial organizations, there is no dispute over goals and performance. Changes in market valuations and profitability (such as stock price, earnings per share, and economic value added) are the dominant outcomes. All decisions are made (at least theoretically under rational conditions) to maximize these key integrative performance metrics. Since customer satisfaction, quality, and operations all need to be aligned to maximize one of these metrics, and since these firms are all attempting to maximize profits, they are very good metrics for understanding the organization's overall health. That works well in many industries.

Hospitals and health systems, however, are different for several reasons, which makes it difficult to apply one singular metric:

1. More than 85% of all healthcare systems are not for profit in nature and seek to improve the public's health. If we tried to simply use financial performance as the outcome, this ignores a dominant mission.
2. Clinical and service quality often takes many years to become transparent to patients and payers. Although we are seeing many government agencies begin to push self-regulation and self-reporting of quality metrics, this is only in its infancy. Programs from both public and private organizations, such as the U.S. Department of Health and Human Services Agency for Healthcare Research and Quality (AHRQ), the Joint Commission, the National Association for Healthcare Quality, and the National Committee for Quality Assurance, are all making good strides toward quality reporting. Unfortunately, the transparency and visibility of these quality data have a lower impact on current performance than in other industries.
3. Health systems are often required to take on charitable or indigent care, which obviously significantly impacts financials.

Figure 2.2   Strategic performance.

4. Healthcare organizations are investing aggressively in new medical technologies and research—which hopefully will pay off in terms of clinical outcomes in later years, but often has a significantly negative impact on short-run performance.

Therefore, a useful performance framework for healthcare will integrate multiple aspects of financial performance, as shown in Figure 2.2.

Each of the core dimensions of performance (i.e., quality, strategic and financial, and operational) influences the others; they are interrelated. If you make changes in some, this impacts the others, either positively or negatively. Also, the relative importance that each organization places on each dimension varies—some organizations focus most of their efforts on clinical quality, while some might be focused on financials or operations. This depends on several factors, such as their current state of affairs, the level of market turbulence, or the phase of the organization's life cycle. Finally, notice that there are quite a few variables or indicators in each performance dimension. There are probably quite a few more that are not listed, but these are the primary ones.

There needs to be a mechanism to allow managers to comprehensively understand the performance of their organization. Reports, financial statements, and other text-based assessments are often too time-consuming. What has emerged is the idea of a visual aid to see the key metrics of an organization.

One type of visual tool for managers is a balanced scorecard. A *balanced scorecard* is a set of measures that gives top managers a fast and comprehensive view of the organization's performance (Kaplan and Norton, 1992). The balanced scorecard recognizes that financial and operating metrics are always intertwined, so it is important to measure them simultaneously to understand their effects on each other and overall for the organization. This has also been applied in healthcare organizations for some time, and has been shown to provide significant benefits (Inamdar et al., 2002; Zelman et al., 2003). Use of a balanced scorecard in performance improvement will

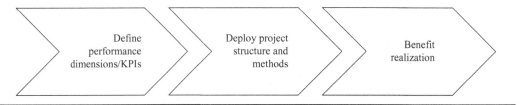

Figure 2.3   Achieving project benefits.

help to guide key measures and encourage alignment from one project team to another. Scorecards are also called dashboards.

For every project that a quality and performance improvement analyst undertakes, there *must* be a primary focus. At the planning stages, performance improvement analysts should identify which performance dimension this project is most likely to impact. The first stage of process improvement or project management starts with either a prioritization or "business case," but in many cases, the measures of improvement are very qualitative, "soft," and intangible. Performance analysts should get to a deeper understanding of potential performance impacts prior to project kickoff, so that the project can be mapped out with this in mind. Unfortunately, many healthcare organizations ignore this stage, and then question why they did not realize any benefits.

Absent defined performance criterion, quality coordinators should make their initial effort focused on defining performance dimensions, specific KPIs, and then ensuring that the project is developed and managed to eventually lead toward improvement in those areas. Figure 2.3 shows the link between up-front planning and performance impact, to benefit realization.

Change versus Improvement

All projects that a performance improvement analyst undertake will have one of two forms: they are either exploratory or change oriented. In many cases, however, even exploratory projects eventually become focused on change. *Change* is a transition from one state to another, or a process of becoming different. Change is not always for the better, but it is always different. Project professionals should *not* focus on achieving change for change's sake, but rather focus on making things better. *Improvement* is positive change or a transition from something in a steady state to something better. Improvement adds value and delivers benefits in the expected performance dimension and specific KPI.

As each project is undertaken, keeping the differences between change and improvement in mind is especially important. Projects, whether focused on process improvement or technology implementation, deliver change to people's work environments and processes. They may even impact their livelihood or that of their colleagues.

Improvement is relative. That is, improvement cannot become an absolute change across all projects for all measures. It must be defined in the initial project planning phase, with an understanding of where the existing performance is, what level of resources and investment will be made, and the time frame provided. These three variables (current performance, resources, and timeline) determine the relative improvements that can be made in any dimension.

Strategy and Performance

Performance improvement is tightly coupled with business strategy. Most healthcare organizations engage in a strategic planning process to develop a strategy. As described in Chapter 1, *strategy* represents the direction and choice of a unique and valuable position rooted in systems of activities that are much more difficult to match (Porter, 1996). Alternatively, it is a path to move from where organizations are today to where they want to be in the future. We will use the term *strategy* here synonymously with *business strategy* and *organizational strategy*. These are terms related to the highest levels of an organization, not single departments or functions. Both of these positions (current vs. future) are measured in terms of performance, whether it is market share, clinical quality, patient satisfaction, or profitability. The mission of performance improvement is therefore to enable strategy.

The process of achieving a strategy in healthcare is rarely as simple as one giant leap in a specific area; rather, it is a collection of small improvements in a number of domains. In other words, if a hospital's primary strategy is to "improve brand and competitive position," then there might be a dozen or more initiatives that will have to be developed to achieve the strategy. Figure 2.4 shows the relationship between strategy, initiatives, and projects.

As this figure shows, improvements in a number of areas have to be made before strategic shifts can be seen in organizational performance. Setting performance objectives is typically one of the first processes in

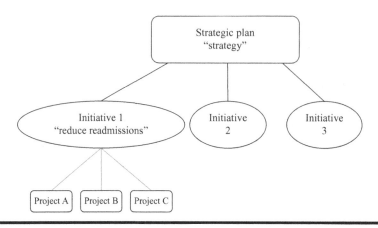

Figure 2.4 Strategy and improvement are aligned.

strategic planning. In many ways, performance improvement consultants working on a project might have their performance targets dictated to them as a result of the strategic plans. In other environments, the plans simply serve as the framework for setting priorities and target areas. Figure 2.5 shows a typical process of strategic planning and highlights where performance targets come into play.

Performance-Based Planning

Since all projects involve a focus on a specific outcome metric, all projects need to essentially start by using a performance-driven planning approach. This requires that the management analyst assemble the project team and clarify goals and objectives. Leading questions should be used, such as

Figure 2.5 Setting performance targets.

- Where are we trying to go? Where are we moving from?
- Which performance dimension are we the weakest in? Which ones are we strongest in?
- What are our competition or benchmark organizations doing in this area? Are we behind them or leading them?
- If we make a change in one performance area, will it impact others that we should be aware of?
- How will these improvements impact patient satisfaction?
- Do we really know our current performance levels?
- Have we seen the measures graphically represented over time? Can we all agree on trends?

After these questions have thoroughly been explored, it becomes much easier to develop a common purpose for the project, and to align the team around expectations and goals. This stage often takes considerable time, several hours per day for a week or longer—possibly more for really large projects, such as an enterprise resource planning (ERP) system implementation.

Once these high-level plans are initiated, the next step is to focus on performance specifics. These include asking questions such as

- What specific definition are we going to use for the metric? Although this may seem basic, it is necessary to apply a standardized and consistent definition to ensure comparability across other organizations and over time. The definition needs to be understood and embraced by all, so that it cannot be manipulated over the project to ensure project success.
- Where can we find existing data sources? What systems, either manual or electronic, exist?
- If there are no existing sources of data, what investigational method will we use to measure current performance? (e.g., pilot project to identify process costs, observe waiting times, or collect quality indicators)
- How long of a time period are we going to look back and forward? A minimum of six months before and after is normally of sufficient length, but many projects wish to look two or three years out.

Notice that all this comes planning comes before a specific method or tool is even discussed. One of the common problems is that a performance improvement analyst walks in the room with his Six Sigma tool kit or plan-do-check-act (PDCA) methodology, but the first set of tasks is oriented not toward methods but discovery. *Discovery* is a thorough investigation of the present environment and collection of evidence. Discovery also requires that a thorough assessment be applied to understand performance relative to best practices. Once the discovery occurs, a method can be applied based on the unique goals and challenges brought forth in the discovery. In essence, one tool or method cannot be applied to all projects.

One of the useful tools for discovery is the diagnostic assessment, which is created custom for each project. The assessment helps to quantitatively assess performance along a number of different process dimensions: personnel, technology, management systems, existing performance metrics, and many others. It requires the management engineer to do some initial work to help research and catalog best practices for the specific process or department, but it is invaluable to help prioritize work efforts and set the initial foundation. A sample diagnostic assessment for a generic process is shown in Figure 2.6.

Assessments such as these should be customized for each process and collectively evaluated by the group in order to provide project alignment and focus.

Setting Performance Targets

Within this framework, healthcare managers must find a way to define and align projects toward these performance dimensions, to enable the strategy. These could be automation and information systems, new building development, implementation of new service lines, or something entirely different.

Best practice/objective	Evaluation				
	1	2	3	4	5
1. Process has clear metrics and is routinely measured					
2. A technology plan exists for integrating the process					
3. Work is highly manual					
4. Participants understand the global (not just local) tasks					
5. Process trends are understood by administrators					
6. Productivity metrics are established and measurable					
7. Outsourcing is used as appropriate					
8. A contingency/backup system exists					
9. Staffing is aligned with demand					
10. Trends and metrics for accrued salaries are analyzed					
11. Employees are well trained in process					
12. There is a strong focus on customer service					
13. There is a strong focus on cycle time					
14. Errors and rework are measured and minimized					
15. Employees understand the direction and key goals					

Figure 2.6   Diagnostic assessment sample.

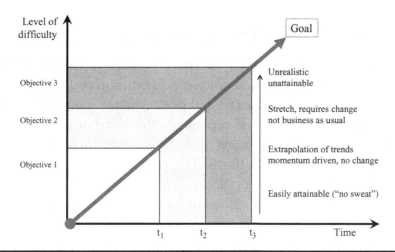

Figure 2.7   Goal setting and level of difficulty.

When the strategy has been established, the projects are defined, and the current performance levels are known, goals and objectives need to be established.

While these two terms—*goals* and *objectives*—are often used interchangeably, they are different. *Goals* are broad, long-term statements of an ideal future state. For instance, the elimination of diabetes is a very long-term goal. *Objectives* are more specific, short-term, quantifiable statements that are readily measurable. An example of an objective would be a 2.5% reduction in hospital-acquired infection rates.

Goals and objectives help to transform the current performance level and path. With the introduction of a change (new project or system), the existing trend is shifted and results in new, hopefully more positive, improvements in performance levels.

While goals are typically broad and not easily measured on a periodic basis, objectives are. Objectives represent specific targets for managers and performance improvement analysts that should be tailored to individual projects. Setting performance targets is often difficult, however. If the project manager sets them too lofty, they are unachievable and might de-motivate staff and team members. If they are too easy, they deliver only marginal value for the organization. Achieving the right balance is key, where they are "stretch" goals that encourage positive change, deliver substantial value, and motivate team members. Figure 2.7 shows the differences between goals and objectives, and how levels impact difficulty.

Also remember the guidelines discussed earlier. All performance targets must be measurable, quantifiable, consistent, and reliable indicators over time for that performance dimension.

EMERGENCY DEPARTMENT CASE STUDY

A project has been undertaken by the emergency department (ED) at Coles-Bart Regional Hospital, a mid-sized community hospital in urban Georgia, to improve a key operational performance metric: leave without being seen (LWBS) rates. LWBS represents the number of times a patient left the ED without actually being seen by a healthcare provider. This is usually due to excessive wait times. The primary factor that initiated the project was patient complaints, and a concern by ED management that their current capacity was insufficient to handle their daily demand for accidents, trauma, and other emergencies.

Lucy Bobs was assigned the role of project manager. Lucy is an industrial engineer by training, and is assigned to the performance solutions department. Lucy's manager informed her that the ED was especially "political" and influential, and that she needed to work very closely with the personnel to ensure they remained satisfied.

Lucy assembled the team, comprised of the ED administrator, a surgeon, a nurse manager, and herself, to assess the situation. She asked the ED administrator if she could view the current performance metrics for the department, and discovered that there was a lack of any documented metrics. She was told that the project should not be slowed down as a result of this. Lucy pushed to try to define an "ideal" environment, which would make the participants satisfied. The team discussed and debated this for some time, and finally defined the ideal environment as one in which "patients move seamlessly through the perioperative period with no delays." This was promptly written down as the vision of the project.

The chief of emergency services, however, continued to offer his perspective that what the department really needed was a new technology system called ED Fantasy. This software would provide graphical reports that could be displayed in the halls and would eliminate use of manual rosters and shift schedules. He had seen the system at one of the most recent conferences he had attended. The system was discussed, competitive options were explored, and then the vendor was called for pricing.

Soon thereafter, the purchasing department was contacted to put a request for proposal (RFP) out on the street, and after 60 days, a license agreement was in place. Implementation started soon after, and ED Fantasy went live nearly 180 days after that.

Following completion of the project, Lucy was asked to write a summary document that described the success of the project. She described the project as having a total duration of 250 days (well under the 365-day average project duration), rapid implementation of new technology, and satisfied ED stakeholders. Overall, Lucy considered this a very successful project.

In this case study, the performance improvement analyst did a reasonably good job in many respects: she obviously helped to keep up the team's momentum, helped achieve some level of perceived success, and kept the team intact, which is sometimes quite a feat. However, there are also many lessons we can learn from what Lucy failed to do properly. She failed to perform any benchmarking, she allowed the primary sponsor to direct the efforts solely toward a technology solution, and she viewed the project too narrowly in terms of expectations. All these can be overcome by following the guidelines and suggestions offered below.

Benchmarking

One way to establish benefit or performance targets is to benchmark against other hospitals or health systems. *Benchmarking* is the comparison of a key performance measurement relative to that of the competition or other leading organizations. It can also be defined as the process of seeking best practices among better-performing organizations, with intentions of applying those internally.

There are a number of different types of benchmarking—those that focus on process, services, best practices, or competition. In most respects, however, the purpose is the same (to compare and assess), but its specific focus or unit of analysis is different. For example, suppose that there are five hospitals in the same large, urban city. The chief nursing officer of one of the hospitals hired a performance engineer to help analyze how overall nursing productivity (measured as number of total procedures performed divided by the nursing labor time) compares with that of the other four organizations. At a high level, the analyst could simply look up the labor and volume data historically, using secondary published data available from the American Hospital Directory or the American Hospital Association. Doing this provides a baseline comparison that can be analyzed over time to get trends. This would be a good example of competitive benchmarking, where the best practice organizations can be identified and further reviewed. If the analyst were to call the other sites, ask for a walk-through of the floors or units, and observe the functions in detail, this would be a good example of process benchmarking.

There are both limitations and advantages to using primary and secondary data in benchmarking. Obviously, direct interviews and observations are typically better than using secondary data in some respects, since the data are more real time and allows for feedback and communication about definitions and metrics. Primary data, however, also have their own limitations, such as the interviewee giving biased or skewed responses, based on his or her interpretations of questions, or simply wanting to make his or her process seem superior to that of others.

Probably the best way we've found to collect performance benchmarking data is to use best practice organizations in other cities, to avoid competitive concerns about the sharing of data. The process is fairly straightforward, with five steps: identify problems and gaps, identify best practice organizations, prepare for a visit, conduct a site visit, and adopt practices into the organization.

Identify Problems and Gaps

Identify the specific problem area, whether it is a process concern or a performance gap. Then, clearly document the problem and define the current process capabilities. Process capabilities include analysis of the historical data and trends and use of a capability index (such as C_{pk}, described in Chapter 3), using statistical analyses of the transactional or performance data, if at all possible.

Research and Identify Best Practice Organizations

Conduct a search, using published data or library searches, of those organizations that appear to have best practices. Ideally, these should be the organizations that have established themselves as leaders in the specific area you are focusing on. The use of newsletters, journals, magazines, or case studies is often one way to find these best practices. Once identified, the organization should be contacted and a site visit requested. Other potential resources for data include the following associations, organizations, and agencies:

1. Healthcare Information and Management Systems Society (www.himss.org)
2. American College of Healthcare Executives (www.ache.org)
3. Healthcare Financial Management Association (www.hfma.org)
4. American Medical Informatics Association (www.amia.org)
5. National Quality Forum (www.qualityforum.org)
6. Agency for Healthcare Research and Quality (www.ahrq.gov)
7. National Association for Healthcare Quality (www.nahq.org)
8. National Committee for Quality Assurance (www.ncqa.org)
9. Centers for Medicare and Medicaid Services (www.cms.hhs.gov)
10. Joint Commission (www.jointcommission.org)
11. DNV Healthcare (http://dnvglhealthcare.com)
12. American Hospital Directory (www.ahd.com)
13. American Hospital Association (www.aha.org)
14. ProQuest ABI/Inform (www.proquest.com)
15. National Institute for Health and Excellence, United Kingdom (www.nice.org.uk)

Prepare for Benchmarking Visit

Prepare detailed plans for what you hope to gain from the visit. Preparation is key, and is often minimized. Adequate preparation ensures that a full set of questions are developed, a plan for how to spend the time with the host is constructed and shared, and both parties understand the goals and objectives for the visit. Showing up at a benchmarking site with no plan is a waste of a lot of resources. Questions will obviously vary by site and by process. For an evaluation of a new information system, where best practices of the implementation are to be analyzed, some generic questions could include those listed in Table 2.2.

Conduct Site Visit

The next step is to conduct the actual site visit. This is when the preparation from the previous step is executed. It is important to bring the right people to the visit, and assign people to take detailed notes and collect any documentation necessary for follow-up. During the visit, observing firsthand the

Table 2.2   Potential Questions for Information System Benchmarking Visit

1. What was the projected benefit versus the amount realized? What was the primary reason for the variances?
2. Which one system drives most of the business value?
3. What is an estimate of the total cost? How much of this was planned versus unexpected?
4. What are some of your biggest lessons learned?
5. If you could do it over again, what would you do differently?
6. What are you least proud of in the implementations?
7. Which task on the project timeline took significantly more resources or time than you estimated? How many people were involved in the overall project? How many were dedicated 100%?
8. Which vendors did you select? Why were they chosen?
9. What was the total project timeline? Was it far off from the original projection?
10. What was the overall reaction by your staff in the beginning (e.g., positive, negative, or indifferent)? Why?
11. What were the three greatest improvements in actual performance indicators or process capabilities?
12. Were there any technical or system glitches we should be aware of?
13. What surprises did you encounter?
14. What role did consultants play in this process?
15. Can we see an example of the system?
16. Do you have any performance scorecards we could look at?

participants, events, activities, and systems in the process being reviewed is critical, in addition to getting all the questions addressed that help you to understand the best practice and adopt it after benchmarking.

Adopt and Integrate Best Practices

After the visit, it is important to gather the benchmarking team, discuss findings, document the best practices, and most importantly, incorporate these into the plans and process changes immediately. Adapting the best practices and adopting them as your own is the only way that benchmarking proves to be a valuable exercise.

Guidelines for Performance Management

Achieving improvement is difficult, even in the best of conditions. The following are guidelines or recommendations for how performance improvement consultants can use their project to deliver value to the organization: define success carefully, measure historical performance, forecast the desired improvement target, and believe you are the expert.

Define Success More Carefully

One of the most common problems in process improvement work is that the initial task of defining desired performance is often cut short. Administrators in healthcare tend to believe they already know what problem exists and where they want to go, without any careful analysis or discovery of facts. More than any other industry, healthcare also tends to define performance very abstractly and broadly, which makes it easy to claim success in post-project evaluations, but very difficult to prove.

The initial effort in this case study needed to select a performance dimension and associated set of KPIs right from the beginning. Collaboratively, the group needed to spend the appropriate amount of time brainstorming and planning desired performance impacts: Would a project impact quality, financials, operations, or a combination? Which specific metric? In many cases, there has been virtually no planning around performance indicators, and so when a project for a technology or process is initiated, the first step has to be to carefully plan. It is easy to skip this step, but then all that a project can really claim is that it delivered change, not improvement.

Measure Historical Performance

Once the team identified or developed the ideal performance criteria, there needed to be effort to develop a methodology for collecting and analyzing the data behind that indicator. For example, assume it was waiting times for patients. Without an understanding of current levels of wait periods, how can an organization suggest that any improvements were made post-project? That is what happens in many cases: organizations suggest that they don't have the right system or process in place to measure current results, so only after the project is successful can they begin to measure. That is flawed thinking.

In industrial organizations, only those projects are undertaken that deliver results. To prove results, one must measure the delta, or change, between pre- and post-project metrics. This thinking has to become more customary in healthcare if real improvements are to be made. Industrial engineers, project managers, and performance improvement professionals all play a pivotal role in helping make this a reality.

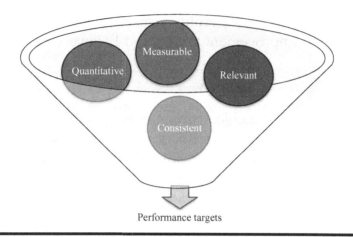

Performance targets

Figure 2.8   Criteria for improvement targets.

Forecast the Desired Improvement Target

Once the performance indicator is established, and historical data are collected, a target must be created to show the desired direction and level for that criterion. If it is waiting times, and historically the operating room showed a 1.6-hour wait presurgery, then the project needs to make a reasonable target for future performance. Ideally, this should be staged based on timing. For example, "in the first six months post-project, wait times will decrease 30% to 67 minutes." That way, the desired performance target is

- ◼ *Measurable*, in both absolute and relative terms
- ◼ *Quantitative*, using precise percentage changes numerically
- ◼ *Consistent*, with existing definitions and data over multiple periods
- ◼ *Relevant*, by using the right performance dimension

Figure 2.8 summarizes the keys to setting performance targets.

Believe You Are the Expert

As the quality and performance improvement professional, it is up to you to ensure that the project does the right thing—that is, the group follows a methodology, applies rigor consistently, and ensures that projects focus on results, outcomes, and positive change or improvement. As the expert, the performance improvement analyst must use his or her expert authority to guide the project in the right direction over the long run.

In larger organizations, politics or bureaucracy will always impede projects. However, if the performance improvement professional does the right thing, is trained in the right methodology, is diligent about results, and facilitates effectively, "impeding" will not lead to "preventing" project success.

Don't Let Benefits Leak Out

Performance gains do accrue to successful projects, but even those that are meticulously planned and executed have some benefit leakage. According to Mankins and Steele (2005), only 63% of the total potential performance gains are realized by most organizations. Performance losses occur because of inadequate resources, poor strategy, lack of accountability, lack of monitoring, and many other reasons. Using the right methods, for the right project, and maintaining a perspective focused on pre- and post-performance is key to maintaining those performance gains over the long term.

Summary

Performance is multidimensional. Health systems are here to survive, to provide valuable services to the community, to improve patient outcomes, and to achieve other strategic, operational, and clinical value. Quality management and performance improvement analysts are often tasked with leading projects, and a critical (often overlooked) step is to carefully define the performance criteria to be impacted before undertaking the project. Benefits can never be realized from a project or process change if the initial planning about performance does not occur, and if precise performance measures are not collected for the past and projected into the future. Performance improvement analysts play a critical role in delivering value to the modern health system, but they must do the right things and do things right.

Key Terms

Balanced scorecard, benchmarking, change, discovery, goals, improvement, key performance indicator (KPI), mission accountability, mortality, morbidity, objectives, performance management, strategy

Discussion Questions

1. What are the core components of performance management?
2. How does your organization's strategy impact the type of performance improvement projects you work on?
3. What level of difficulty should you use when setting goals and objectives?
4. Which type of performance indicator do you feel is the most important in healthcare?

References

Inamdar N, Kaplan RS, and Bower M (2002). Applying the balanced scorecard in healthcare provider organizations. *Journal of Healthcare Management*, 47(3), 195–196.

Kaplan RS and Norton D (1992). The balanced scorecard: Measures that drive performance. *Harvard Business Review*, 70(1), 71–79.

Langabeer J (2009). *Performance Improvement in Hospitals and Health Systems*. Chicago: Healthcare Information and Management Systems Society.

Langabeer J and Helton J (2016). *Healthcare Operations Management: A Systems Perspective*. Boston: Jones and Bartlett Publishers.

Mankins MC and Steele R (2005). Turning great strategy into great performance. *Harvard Business Review*, 83(8), 64–72.

Porter M (1996). What is strategy? *Harvard Business Review*, November/December 1996, 61–80.

Sadhegi S, Barsi A, Mikhail O, and Shabot M (2012). *Integrating Quality and Strategy in Health Care Organizations*. Boston: Jones and Bartlett Publishers.

Zelman W, Pink G, and Matthias C (2003). Use of the balanced scorecard in healthcare. *Journal of Healthcare Finance*, 29(4), 1–16.

PERFORMANCE IMPROVEMENT METHODS

The path toward better quality and performance is boosted by following a structured methodology with appropriate tools and techniques. Yet, there are multiple choices of methods and complex decisions to be made, especially for new analysts. How performance improvement is organized, managed, and evaluated establishes how successful the group is going to be. In this part, we focus on how to create a new organization focused on performance improvement, how to better manage it (including selection of projects and monitoring of results), and how to apply the basics of process redesign and project management. We discuss how to best establish and lead a performance improvement department. We have seen a resurgence of focus and energy around performance improvement, and many new teams are being developed. We discuss project intake and evaluation methods, focused on maximizing outcomes for your portfolio of projects, and aligning the right methods to these projects. We focus on some of the unique ways to help show the value and concepts behind management engineering groups.

This part also details the basics of both project management and change management. Achieving project success is often only possible when the engineer develops "softer" skills—such as communication and facilitation—and understanding these qualitative aspects of a project are usually just as important as the technical components. We also describe some insight into how to avoid common pitfalls in dealing with organizational change.

Chapter 3

Performance Management Methods and Tools

James Langabeer

Contents

A bad system will beat a good person every time.

Dr. W. Edwards Deming
Quality Guru

Introduction

The choice of which performance management methodology to adopt is a critical one. Multiple methods exist, from plan–do–check–act (PDCA) to Six Sigma, Lean, and theory of constraints (TOC), to name just a few. Each method has its own goal, tools, and approach. In this chapter, we explore the methodologies and the tools and techniques underlying these methods.

Quality Measures

Dr. Avedis Donabedian (a physician and quality outcomes pioneer) created a conceptual model that defines how healthcare outcomes and performance can be improved. The *Donabedian model* is a structural framework for examining quality of care (Figure 3.1).

As shown in Figure 3.1, this model implies that the inputs (or underlying structure of an organization and its environment) determine how providers and administrators in an organization will act. Structure includes all types of resources, such as facilities, technology and systems, finances, and personnel.

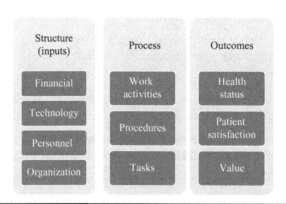

Figure 3.1 Donabedian model.

The Donabedian model helped to frame quality and performance outcomes in healthcare (Donabedian, 2005). Consequently, there are different types of measures for structure, process, and outcomes.

Structural Measures

Structural outcomes are those that define the capacity or infrastructure in healthcare. For example, nurse staffing ratios (number of nurses per patient in a hospital) are one common structural measure. Adoption of health information technology (such as an electronic health record) is another common structural measure.

Process Measures

Structure impacts process. A *process* is a linked set of activities necessary to achieve a goal or produce a deliverable. Process describes how work is accomplished. In healthcare, this includes clinical activities (such as diagnosis and treatment), but also administrative processes (such as how payments are made). Process determines outcomes to a large degree. Outcomes include better health status, functioning, quality of life, patient satisfaction, and value.

Process measures are those that describe the quality, volume, and performance of a clinical or business process. For example, a process measure could include whether a patient was provided aspirin on admission or discharge (as in the case of patients with cardiovascular disease), or adherence rates to specific medications. Process of care measures reflect the quality of care provided to patients in an organization.

Outcome Measures

Better processes produce better results. To improve processes, organizations should adopt a formalized approach to mapping out processes and looking for ways to streamline and simplify them. Outcome measures reflect the output of a process. An output measure can be as straightforward as mortality rate (e.g., survival to hospital discharge or in-hospital mortality). Readmission rates and rates of surgical or hospital-acquired infections are also very common institutional measures of outcomes. Other outcomes are disease specific, such as case-mix adjusted length of stay for acute myocardial infarction.

Finally, there are composite quality measures. Composite implies that they are summary measures, either for an organization or for a specific disease condition (e.g., sepsis, stroke, heart failure, or diabetes). Typically, composite measures are a small subset of the most significant metrics for a disease. The National Quality Forum (www.qualityforum.org) maintains an active list of all quality metrics endorsed by various organizations and associations (National Quality Forum, 2017). *Healthcare Effectiveness Data and Information Set* (HEDIS) is one standardized database of quality measures used to assess physicians and providers across the country, and it is used by insurance providers and health plans to report and benchmark quality (National Commitee for Quality Assurance, 2017). HEDIS provides specific operational definitions for metrics, to ensure the consistency of reported measures. The National Committee for Quality Assurance maintains the active list of HEDIS quality measures (www.ncqa.org).

There are many other measure sets in existence. Hospitals and provider groups are often confused by which types of measures to embrace. There are literally several hundred different measures in use by organizations, health plans, and insurers. This is further confounded by professional societies that endorse their own disease-specific measures, such as diabetes or cancer. The Centers for Medicare and Medicaid Services (CMS) is one of the largest payers in care, through the Medicare and Medicaid programs. CMS is trying to bring clarity to quality measures, by reimbursing patients for their achievement of quality. Programs such as the Merit-based Incentive Payment System (MIPS) are quality programs that reimburse providers for quality (instead of quantity), and are a move toward *value-based payment* models. Value-based payment is an approach used by payers to ensure that providers focus on quality and value, and not just quantity, which will be discussed in more detail in Chapter 9.

Plan–Do–Check–Act

The most basic four-step methodology for continuous improvement is known as PDCA, or alternatively as plan–do–study–act (PDSA). Both PDCA and PDSA refer to the same basic process, and have a focus on continuously refining results over time and incorporating those learnings into the system. PDCA is a methodology for continuous improvement.

Plan. This refers to the development of the guidelines, framework, and goals to achieve specific targets. Appropriate measures should be identified that are high priority and in need of improvement. Quantitative expectations should be developed for these measures as well.

Do. This phase represents the execution or implementation of the plan, whether that is implementation of a revised process or adoption of a new application. This involves applying specific improvement methods to work toward desired targets for each measure. Data collection and analysis are also part of this phase.

Check. This can also be referred to as "study." In this phase, we measure and evaluate the data collected earlier against the plans. Statistical process control and other tools are often used to assess the behavior of processes and to explore variations and trends in outcomes.

Act. In this phase, refinement and adjustments to the process should continue. If the process has achieved desired effects in a test environment, then these will be put into the full system. Some organizations first deploy small pilots to test feasibility. A *pilot* is a small-scale project used to test results before widespread deployment. It is extremely useful to ensure that all kinks are worked out, in both technology and process.

Six Sigma

One useful tool for analyzing a process is a *flowchart*. A flowchart is a visual diagram depicting the sequential actions, steps, inputs, and decisions in a process. Since most processes require information or physical flows between departments or even organizations, they can be displayed with or without swim lanes. A swim lane is a depiction of the boundaries between processes and the cross-functionality between various parties in order to execute the business process. These can be either horizontally or vertically

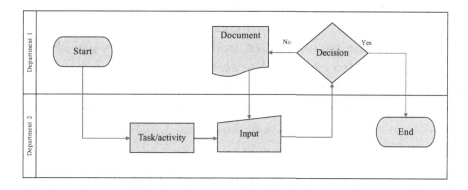

Figure 3.2   Process flowchart.

displayed. A sample process flowchart with a few of the key symbols is shown in Figure 3.2, presented with horizontal swim lanes.

Six Sigma is a quality improvement method focused on eliminating defects and reducing variability through statistical process control. It gained significant attention because of the work of industrial organizations such as Motorola and General Electric (Pyzdek and Keller, 2014). The primary advantage of this method is its focus on variance reduction or reduced variability. It is an approach to solving problems that requires users to focus on the primary measures, and to improve their problem solving and decision making to get there.

First thing you might ask is, why is it called Six Sigma? *Sigma* is the mathematical term for standard deviation, annotated by the Greek symbol σ. Standard deviation is defined as the square root of the variance. What we know about managing process behavior is that if we seek a reduction in variability, we want most measures to hover around the average (also called mean and typically represented by the Greek symbol $\bar{x}$). For example, if it takes on average 20 minutes to perform a catheterization in an interventional cardiac laboratory, we ideally would want all cases to take around 20 minutes, not wide swings in either direction. In the optimal sense, assuming that the patient's underlying condition was the same (which I realize is a difficult assumption to make), then we want the first and the last case to be relatively the same in terms of process behavior and outcomes. Processes that are "in control" do not have wide swings and variation, so that one time it is two hours and the next it is 20 minutes. Reducing variation and consistency are the goals.

Standard deviation is the primary statistical measures of variability or dispersion in data observations. In a normally distributed set of data, ±1 standard deviation from the mean will include 68.2% of all observations, and two standard deviations represent 95% of all observations. *Normal distributions* of data have a larger, denser concentration of observations toward the center and less on the sides (called tails). This assumes that we have enough observations, of course. Statistically, we can ensure that data are normal when we calculate the mean, median, and mode, and they are identical or nearly identical. We also can calculate *skewness* (or asymmetry of the data) and *kurtosis* (heavily tailed in one direction or another) and ensure that both values are within normally defined ranges (usually +2 to −2) (Figure 3.3).

DMAIC

Six Sigma has a five-step cycle for improvement: DMAIC. DMAIC is an acronym for define, measure, analyze, improve, control. This is very similar

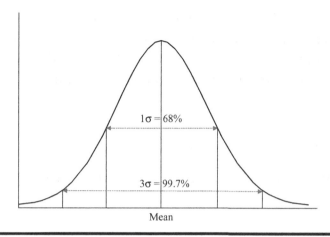

Figure 3.3   Normal distribution and sigma.

in nature to the PDSA or PDCA process, but focuses heavily on the up-front definition and measurement phase. It also places much more emphasis on statistical calculations and measurements. *Define* refers to understanding the problem, and specifically defining what is wrong with it: Is it not meeting customer requirements? Does it have excessive wait times? Are employees or stakeholders unhappy? Defining the problem is the first step toward improving it.

Measure is the quantification of the problem. It starts by exploring where current performance measures are, and where they should be. *Analyze* requires a thorough understanding of the cause of the problem. Fishbone diagrams, Pareto analyses, process analyses, and other techniques are required in this phase.

Improve is phase 4 of the cycle. This step is when the project team recommends solutions and verifies and implements them, at least partially in a pilot, to observe effects. Brainstorming will be incredibly important, which requires good teamwork and listening. *Brainstorming* is a team approach to generating ideas and solving problems. Development of "to be" process maps should also be employed, to contrast again the "as is" maps, and show steps removed and processes changed.

The final step in DMAIC is to *control* the process and maintain a solution that can be operationalized and made stable over time. This requires changes to standard operating procedures, a control plan, and other documentation that codifies the change for employees to follow. It also should expand the solution beyond the pilot if it has not already. Monitoring and routinely reevaluating the performance is essential to the control phase.

Six Sigma suggests that in normal data observations, we seek to minimize the number of sigma deviations away from the mean and to reduce the number of errors in the process. One way to do this is through measurement of actual failure rates, calculated as defects per million opportunities (DPMO).

Managing Defects

DPMO is a calculation of defects observed on average divided by the number of opportunities for defects. The first is the idea of an outcome known as a defect. A *defect* is any instance in a process where the customer requirement has not been met. In the earlier example involving nursing procedures, the outcome was positive (i.e., they were successfully completed in 17 minutes). If, however, it took 22 minutes for the procedures, and the patient was not able to have one of the three procedures completed, it would have been recorded as a defect, since it deviated from the expectation and did not meet the customer's (or patient's) expectations. Another example would be an emergency department wait time. Assuming that a defective process would result in patients waiting more than 15 minutes (as an example), the frequency of visits greater than 15 minutes would be treated as process failures or defects.

Six Sigma uses a metric known as DPMO to understand defect behavior for activities and processes. To calculate DPMO, analysts need to perform these four steps:

Step 1: Identify the process to evaluate, and the specific deliverables produced by the process. In our nursing example, the process is nursing procedures and the deliverables are successful completion of three procedures.

Step 2: Define successful outcomes and defects, and count the total number of opportunities. In our example, we defined the defect earlier. The total opportunities would be defined as (no. of patients)×(no. of procedures)×(frequency). For example, if we had 20 patients, each requiring three procedures twice a day, the total number of opportunities would be 120 (or 20×3×2).

Step 3: Obtain a statistical model of the process. In this step, the engineer should observe all the activities, gather the outcomes (as shown earlier), and statistically model the results, calculating the mean, standard deviation, and control limits. In addition, the total number of defects should be counted and recorded. For example, if the engineer observed all 120 opportunities in one day, and counted eight defects (or instances that did not conform to requirements), then the DPMO would be calculated as $(8 \div 120) \times 1,000,000 = 66,667$. Therefore, in this example, the DPMO would be 66,667 (0.06667×10^6).

Step 4: Measure sigma level and manage improvements. After calculating the DPMO, it is compared with a Six Sigma level in order to obtain a measure of improvement opportunities. Six Sigma actually refers to the calculation where only 3.4 defects per million are recorded, which yields a 99.99966% success rate. This yield can be calculated by subtracting from 100% the defect rate (e.g., $100\% - [3.4/1,000,000] = 100 - 0.00034 = 0.9996$ 6, or 99.9%). Figure 3.4 allows you to graphically compare your process's defect rates against sigma and DPMO levels. Using the example from earlier (with more than 66,000 DPMOs), this would indicate sigma level 3.

Process Capability Index

One other useful analytical tool that Six Sigma has provided us is the process capability index (often expressed as C_p). A *process capability index* is a measure for gauging the extent to which a process meets the customer's expectations. Calculating it requires knowledge of the upper and lower control limits on the process behavior. It is mathematically defined as

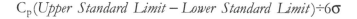

$$C_p (Upper\ Standard\ Limit - Lower\ Standard\ Limit) \div 6\sigma$$

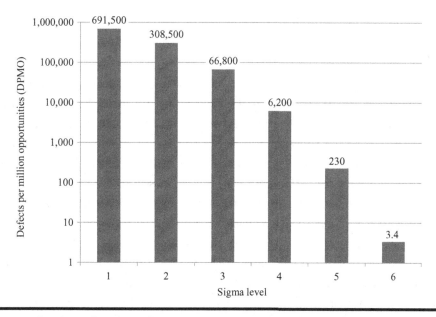

Figure 3.4 Six Sigma levels and DPMO.

$C_p > 1$ suggests that the process is capable, but it does not have any relation to the performance target; it does not suggest that the process meets the customers' expectations. To improve on this, other complementary metrics should be used (such as C_{pk}). C_{pk} is defined as the minimum of either of these formulas:

$$C_p \left[(USL - \bar{x}) \div 3\sigma \right] \quad \text{or} \quad Cp \left[(\bar{x} - LSL) \div 3\sigma \right]$$

Six Sigma Benefits

A few years ago, some colleagues and I performed a systematic review of the Six Sigma results published in peer-reviewed journals over a 15-year period (DelliFraine et al., 2013). What we found was quite interesting. We observed that most of the published accounts of outcomes did not consider changes in pre- versus postperformance of DPMO, process capability index, or any other statistical metric. Results were widely varied, and most did not use numerical values to report the magnitude of change. Although Six Sigma has a wide following, and can work, it needs to be conducted rigorously. There will be benefits to focusing on process variation reduction, and these should be carefully observed and recorded and results should be shared with other organizations to help the industry improve.

Lean

Lean is a quality improvement method focused on removing waste and unnecessary steps from processes. The car manufacturer Toyota in Japan developed Lean. Lean quality management initiatives create standardized and stable processes to provide the best quality services or products as efficiently as possible. Any less than an ideal outcome is investigated immediately in order to identify the root cause and resolve the problem. Lean philosophy embraces a continuous improvement strategy that supports creating simple and direct pathways and eliminating loops and duplication. Lean attempts to aggressively remove all non-value-added activities from a process, meaning any step that does not produce value for the customer or is not essential to producing the final service. The primary approach is to standardize production and business processes so that flow can be leveled and all waste or inefficiencies removed.

Lean uses different tools and techniques to remove waste and improve quality. A key task is to delineate value-added activities from those that do not add value. Processes should seek to remove the non-value-added steps. Value is defined from the customer's perspective. The method for understanding this is through value streams. *Value stream mapping* is a technique where all tasks and actions in a process are modeled visually to show all activities performed from start to finish. Value stream mapping is used to identify those that add value versus those that do not. It is particularly useful to understand tasks that are performed cross-functionally (across functions).

The key steps involved include preparation for the mapping, data collection for the current process, documentation of the desired future state, and execution of the map. A sample value stream map is shown in Figure 3.5, using the visual symbols common for inventory, information flow, and waste as an example.

Lean has many other tools. *Kanban* is a visual card process (think Post-it notes on a whiteboard) that visually provides process flow and identifies bottlenecks. These cards work off the principle that the brain can process visual information easier than reports or numerical data, so they are often used to trigger changes to process for continuous improvement.

Lean also uses a tool called *5S*. It is called that literally because each step starts with the letter s. Each step in this process helps to create the environment (working conditions) for optimizing value-added activities. The 5S includes

- Sort
- Set in order
- Shine
- Standardize
- Sustain

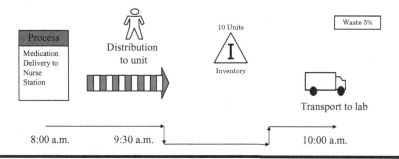

Figure 3.5   Value stream map.

Lean versus Six Sigma

Six Sigma and Lean are often confused, and sometimes combined into Lean Six Sigma. To compare their similarities and differences is important. Overarching goals are fairly similar between both methods, but Lean focuses on doing the right things (value-adding activities), and Six Sigma focuses on doing things right (with no errors). Lean also requires a more traditional methodology centered around Deming's PDSA cycle. Six Sigma relies on DMAIC. Lean utilizes leadership and training roles, such as "sensei" (master teacher), and diffusion of beliefs and cultural value shifts much more than diffusion of analytical techniques. Table 3.1 compares the two methods.

Theory of Constraints

TOC is a quality improvement method that addresses the effect of system constraints on performance outcomes (Goldratt and Cox, 1984). TOC was conceptualized by Dr. Eliyahu Goldratt, a leading quality improvement researcher originally from Israel. TOC primarily has been used to address constraints. A *constraint* is a bottleneck or place where process throughput

Table 3.1 Six Sigma and Lean Comparison

Dimension	*Six Sigma*	*Lean*
Goals	Conformance to customer requirements; elimination of defects (errors, rework)	Remove non-value-added activities; eliminate waste (errors, wait times)
Approach	Reduction of process variability	Standardization, production flow leveling
Principal tool/ method	Statistical process control, run charts, cause-and-effect diagrams	Value stream mapping, Kanban, 5S
Infrastructure	Through formalized structures, titles, and roles	Cultural change; "sensei" relationships
Methodology	DMAIC	PDSA
Performance metrics	Quantifiable, cost of quality; mapped into financial value	Not consistent; often result in new metrics

Source: Langabeer, J., et al., *Operations Management Research*, 2(1), 13–27, 2009.

is limited. TOC focuses on identifying places where constraints occur, and either fixing them or removing them entirely. In this focus on removing bottlenecks, it is similar to Lean's use of Kanban.

Goldratt contends that reducing obstacles that choke throughput will speed up (improve the velocity) of processes, which will result in positive outcomes. There are definitely opportunities in healthcare to explore constraints—everything from wait lines in clinical departments and pharmacies to supply and inventory management concerns. Exploring where personnel shortages, system failures, or lack of products exist is necessary. Targeting the constraint and implementing these changes are key to certain types of improvements, although possibly less so on the clinical side and more on the administrative side. If a process seems to be impacted by issues of throughput, by optimizing supply (available capacity) or demand, then use of a TOC approach would be most suitable.

Process Modeling

Business and clinical processes involve complexities of not only the types of activities involved, but also their timing and handoffs between departments. *Process mapping* is a visual flowchart of ordered activities in a discrete process. It is also commonly called process flow. It starts by comprehensively defining all aspects of the process and placing them in flows on a chart. A sample flowchart was shown earlier in Figure 3.2.

Converting these data into a time period is best done with a run chart. A *run chart* is a line graph of key data plotted over time. Run charts should be used to graphically represent changes in outcomes or important variables over time, to analyze trends and patterns that might emerge. They are especially helpful to plot data to see if changes (a new project or process improvement) have worked, by comparing data over time. They can also help to easily identify if seasonality or other trends emerge. For example, a hospital could plot its data average length of stay (ALOS) metrics by time period (hourly, daily, weekly, monthly, or annually). When you see data presented like this, it helps to easily spot highs and lows and direction of change. Generally speaking, the more granular or detailed the data, the more likely a pattern will emerge that is actionable. Figure 3.6 shows a run chart that plots ALOS by month.

Modeling is the conversion of the process into an analytical model to represent and simulate behaviors given changes in the key components.

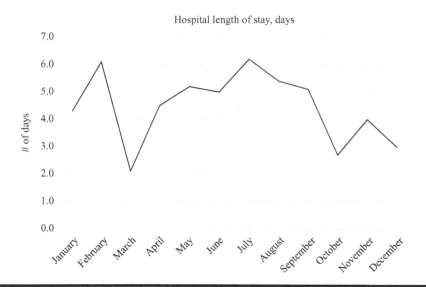

Figure 3.6 Process run chart.

The process model therefore must detail each activity and responsible entity. The components for process modeling should attempt to define each of the following:

- *Activity*: A task that occurs at a specific point in time, has a duration that is random, and shows a known probability distribution function.
- *Time*: Key parameter of a process, defined as the differential between the time an activity started and ended.
- *Resources*: Both inputs and outputs of a process should be defined.
- *Event*: The culmination of an activity, which can change the state of a process.
- *Outcomes*: The results of the activities and events, most commonly expressed in a metric to gauge success and failure.

Most methodologies attempt to model each activity and event, by carefully observing and documenting these components defined above. For example, if a nurse entered a room to take vital signs at 10:05 a.m. and left at 10:22 a.m. with three procedures completed, the output matrix would look like what is shown in Table 3.2.

After adequate observation of these activities, which normally involves a significant period of time, the process can be modeled using traditional process flowchart tools. More importantly, the *behavior* of the activities can be statistically analyzed. This is one of the main contributions of Six Sigma and

Table 3.2   Process Model

Activity	Time	Resources	Event	Outcome
Nurse intervention	17 min, 0 s	Nurse time, 3 units of supply	Nurse completes three procedures	Successful

other data-driven methods. While some may argue that Six Sigma has no role in medicine, we disagree and believe that all processes can benefit from better understanding of their behaviors.

Modeling the time intervals allows engineers to understand the variability of the process. Since variability refers to the degree of dispersion of data points over time, it reflects the range of possible outcomes of a given process. The greater the variability, the less control that exists in the process outcomes. As discussed above, in a normally distributed set of data, ±1 standard deviation from the mean will include 68.2% of all observations. Two standard deviations represent 95% of all observations.

For example, assume we have 11 observations of nursing data, ranging from 11 to 23 minutes. The mean is approximately 17, and the standard deviation of these data is 3.193. Therefore, within 1σ deviation from the mean would be approximately 20.2, and 2σ would (or the 95% confidence interval) would be 23.4 minutes. Therefore, in 68% of the cases, nurses were likely to complete their three procedures between 13.8 and 20.2 minutes. In 95% of the cases, you could expect that nurses would complete their three procedures in no more than 23.4 minutes and no less than 10.6 minutes. Understanding the behavior of data at a statistical level allows engineers to truly understand expectations and map out realistic process models. Figure 3.7 shows the concept of statistical process control graphically.

Software to enable simulation of process modeling is widely available. Tools (e.g., Simul8 and Arena Software) allow for discrete event simulations to be automated, to model key variables (resources and events) to simulate change in outcomes. *Discrete event simulation* is the dynamic modeling of discrete (separate) events to predict overall process and system behaviors. Discrete event simulation works on a graphical layer.

Similarly, Monte Carlo simulation uses mathematical calculations incorporating risk to predict decisions and outcomes. Monte Carlo simulation allows you to use spreadsheets or databases, and is built into a number of software solutions (e.g., Palisade @RISK and Oracle Crystal Ball). Tools such as these allow for multiple iterations and estimations to give better predictions of potential changes in a process.

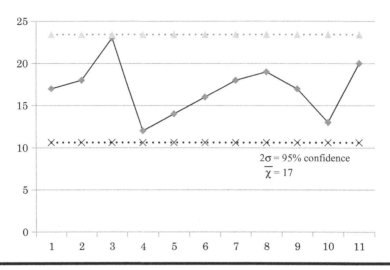

Figure 3.7 Statistical process control.

Other Tools and Techniques

Root cause analysis is an in-depth process or technique for identifying the fundamental factor beneath any variation in performance. *Root cause* is the primary, underlying reason behind an effect (or outcome). Root cause is the primary initiating cause. It is the most basic factor of a specific effect. Root cause analysis should focus quality teams on identifying the underlying mechanisms for poor performance or variation in a process. The emphasis should be on the *process* and *management systems*, not on departments or individuals.

Cause-and-effect analysis is a technique to identify the feasible causes that are related to a specific problem. Typically cause-and-effect diagrams identify all causes of an effect, and then narrow down the analysis to the primary, underlying causes. Cause-and-effect diagrams (also called *fishbone* or Ishikawa) display visually the results of the analysis to make it easier for others to conceptualize and act on them (Figure 3.8).

Failure modes and effects analysis (FMEA) is a tool for documenting potential failures in a process, causes, risks, and potential solutions. FMEA is primarily used to document failures in a process, and clearly specify causes, controls, and actions to mitigate such failures in the future. FMEA is particularly useful when the majority of the poor outcomes (results) are due to a limited number of modes (Figure 3.9).

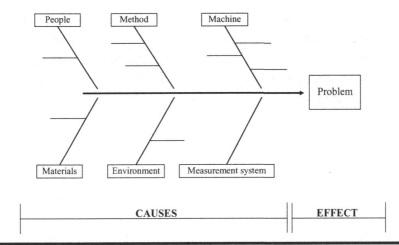

Figure 3.8   Cause-and-effect diagram (fishbone).

Function	Failure mode	Effect	Cause	Controls	Action taken	Owner
Minimize patient wait times	No rooms available	Patient boarded outside room	Lack of rooms	System generated alerts	ED chief to convert private rooms	Jim L.
		Patient wait times excessive	Lack of nursing personnel	Nurse manager manages wait times	Additional personnel recruitment	
		Patient leaves without being seen				

Figure 3.9   Failure modes and effects analysis.

Summary

The Donabedian model helps to provide an underlying framework for explaining how inputs are converted into outputs in healthcare. Structure and process determine outcomes. There are a number of quality methodologies available for health systems to follow to improve performance. The most popular of these include PDCA or PDSA, Six Sigma, Lean, and TOC. Six Sigma is a great analytical tool that uses statistical process control to bring the behavior of processes under control. Lean helps organizations focus on reducing waste and non-value-added activities. TOC works well when you see signs of bottlenecks (or constraints on capacity) that limit your organization to respond to demand responsively. There are a number of process management tools to choose from, including run charts, discrete event simulation, value stream mapping, and Pareto analysis. All of them should be used where most applicable in a process improvement project.

Key Terms

5S, activity, brainstorming, cause-and-effect analysis, constraint, defect, defects per million opportunities (DPMO), discrete event simulation, event, DMAIC, Donabedian model, failure modes and effects analysis, fishbone diagram, HEDIS, Kanban, kurtosis, Lean, modeling, normal distribution, PDCA, pilot, process, process capability index, outcomes, process mapping, resources, root cause, root cause analysis, run chart, sigma, Six Sigma, skewness, standard deviation, time, theory of constraints, value stream mapping, value-based payment, variability

Discussion Questions

1. What does DMAIC stand for?
2. What is the difference between a process of care, structure, and outcome quality measure?
3. Why is the concept of sigma and deviations so important to process control?
4. How does the type of issue your organization faces impact the choice of performance improvement methodology?
5. How is value stream mapping different from process flowcharting?

References

DelliFraine J, Wang M, McCaughey D, Langabeer J, and Erwin C (2013). The use of Six Sigma in healthcare management: Are we using it to its full potential? *Quality Management in Health Care*, 22(3), 210–223.

Donabedian A (2005). Evaluating the quality of medical care. *Milbank Quarterly*, 83(4), 691–729.

Goldratt E and Cox J (1984). *The Goal*. New York: Routledge Publishing.

Langabeer J, DelliFraine J, Heineke J, and Abbass I (2009). Implementation of Lean and Six Sigma quality initiatives in hospitals: A goal theoretic perspective. *Operations Management Research*, 2(1), 13–27.

National Committee for Quality Assurance (2017). Healthcare Effectiveness Data and Information Set (HEDIS) measures. Available at www.ncqa.org.

National Quality Forum (2017). Available at www.qualityforum.org.

Pyzdek T and Keller P (2014). *The Six Sigma Handbook*. 4th edn. New York: McGraw-Hill Education.

Chapter 4

Developing New Quality Teams

James Langabeer

Contents

Quality is everyone's responsibility.

Dr. W. Edwards Deming
Quality Guru

Introduction

Formally organizing a department that focuses on improving processes is very exciting, but also difficult for many reasons. First, very few completely new departments or units are created each year. In a recent survey conducted of healthcare executives, nearly 60% responded that they had a decision support or performance improvement (PI) department already in existence, but most of these departments were less than five people in size, and none were created in the last 12 months (Langabeer et al., 2010). Second, gaining the support and approval of executives, as well as the resource commitment for staff and other expenses, is typically lengthy and time-consuming. Finally, new departments challenge the status quo, and without strong leadership from a sponsor or champion, they tend to fall by the wayside. Yet even if you can get a management engineering or PI team approval, the challenges don't stop there. This chapter outlines some guidelines for how to establish and lead quality management and PI teams.

Building a New Quality or PI Department

Each year, new quality or PI departments are created. Some are just one analyst, and others have a large staff of nurses, engineers, and economists. At large teaching hospitals, which often have more than 10,000 employees, there might even be multiple departments that focus on PI. This happens as organizations become very large and complex, with "silo" structures.

If you are in a position of trying to create a new team or department focused on PI, we can recommend a few steps to help get it approved and functioning quickly. These include development of a business concept, creation of a proposal, gaining executive support, and rolling out the concept.

Develop Business Concept

The first step in the process of creating a new department is a well-thought-out concept or position. A *business concept* clarifies the design or plan for something new. The business concept should describe what the department or team will do, how it will earn revenue (if any), and how it can be used to create organizational value. Sometimes quality departments charge back other areas of the hospital and thus generate revenue, but many times they are solely a cost center. This includes detailing potential benefits, risks, costs, and a vision for what the department would do. Identifying how it is different from the current structure is key to differentiating it from other functions. In some larger facilities, we have seen quality departments under nursing, and PI departments under finance, as an example. They perform largely the same function, yet serve different customers.

Most PI departments focus on one or more of the following areas:

- Project management, such as large systems and facility development
- Process improvement of clinical and support processes
- Decision support, analytics, and modeling for decision making and planning
- Cost-effectiveness and cost–benefit studies
- Performance management, including benchmarking, and scorecard development
- Information technology assessment, implementation, and evaluation
- Operational and business planning

Create Business Case or Proposal

The next step is to begin converting the concept into a proposal that can be exchanged and discussed at multiple levels of the organization. This proposal should contain the traditional aspects of a proposal, such as benefits, business drivers, benchmarks, and resource requirements. Figure 4.1 shows a suggested format for the business.

In order to prepare this proposal correctly, the human resource (HR) components will need to be defined, since HR costs will likely consume 60%–75% or more of the operating budget. Meetings with HR to discuss organizational development, skill profiles of talent (PI professionals), compensation requirements, and a general recruiting strategy should all be

Sponsorship/Champion	• Identify the project sponsor and champion
Business drivers/vision	• Describes the challenges the department could work on • Identify benefit areas • Describe how these opportunities impact performance and contribute to the organization's vision • Describe which division the department will report to
Benefits/outcomes	• Describe the key performance indicators (KPIs) and how the department could impact specific indicators • Document outcomes expectations and improvement areas • Monetarize the "value" of these outcomes over time
Benchmarks	• If possible, outline competitive organizations and their use of similar PI units • Describe implications on organization, policy, and processes
Investment/resource requirements	• Define the proposed investment in terms of staffing, space, technology • Define recommendations for moving forward • List all key assumptions • Document the risks and how they can be mitigated • Define timelines and key milestones

Figure 4.1   Proposing a new PI department.

outlined. Key skills for PI professionals will need to incorporate strong internal consulting background, project management, facilitation, change management, and knowledge of information systems, which is a combination that is often difficult to find in a single person. These details will allow you to phase in the new department over time.

Structure and reporting relationships can represent a tricky situation. Typically, in larger organizations, there are multiple departments in large divisions focused on project management, process improvement, and decision support. These groups can represent barriers or competition, or they can be sources of partnership and collaboration. Deciding how to incorporate them into the vision and concept is critical from the beginning.

Another challenge for many organizations is deciding where to put the PI department. Of course, most PI managers would prefer reporting to the CEO, but we don't see a lot of evidence of that. In many cases, it resides under the chief financial officer (CFO). Sometimes it is a part of information systems. In other organizations, it is embedded in clinical operations or nursing. These are no singular models of success. There can be multiple ways of structuring reporting relationships. What is important is that the executive believes in change and quality and can champion efforts. PI departments can thrive under any of these, as long as they follow the other recommendations.

Gain Executive Consensus and Support

Unless you are the CEO or chairman of the board of trustees, once the proposal has been developed, it will probably require support. The outcomes or benefits you detail in the business case should lay out the argument for potential quality gains. In some organizations, to obtain approval for your business case might only involve talking with your immediate supervisor. But in most organizations today, it requires garnering support from a variety of different executives throughout the organization. In many cases, all the key executives should be given an opportunity to hear the business proposal and offer suggestions and input. This collaborative process of prewiring, as it is called, allows stakeholders to provide input that can be incorporated into subsequent revisions. If these sessions are conducted offline, and not in groups, everybody benefits, and it does not jeopardize the approval process.

One of the more difficult executives to convince of the need is typically the CFO, so it is important that the investment (costs and resources) be outlined clearly and in value terms, so that costs can be compared to gains. Most CFOs like to use net present value (NPV) or other similar time value of money concepts to ensure that total benefits exceed total costs. Doing this in advance, and outlining all assumptions, is very important.

In total, "selling" the concept often takes several months, and requires continuous motivation and discipline to move to the next step.

Rollout Phases

Once support and approval have been gained, the rollout or initiation can begin. Since no organization can go from nothing to fully operational, it is important to use a phased-in approach. Typically, this means an incremental approach, gradually showing value over time.

In the first phase, one might try to develop the vision and mission of the department, plus recruit the key manager for the group. Since recruiting can take 3–12 months, depending on location and many other factors, this first phase could often take a year or longer. Using the management engineering department for our case study, we chose an initial vision to help the institution "discover value opportunities" and use "advanced methods to transform processes and performance throughout the organization."

In the second phase, additional staff must be recruited and educated, methodologies have to be developed or adopted, and tool kits of methods need to be collected. Communication efforts, or marketing, will also need to occur in large institutions, where visibility might not otherwise be possible. E-mail distributions, announcements, or brown-bag seminars to share results of the department's initial projects are necessary for getting wider integration into the organization. In the final stage, as more projects are being requested by departments and other user groups, a process for project "intake" will have to be developed. In Chapter 5 "Project Management," this topic will be discussed more fully. Figure 4.2 shows the phases of development for a new quality or PI department.

Managing PI

Managing quality teams involves both internal analysts and external consultants, and a portfolio of projects in various stages. In the early phase of developing a new department, the focus of management should be on selecting the right individuals, educating them, and then selecting the initial set of methodologies to be used. It is important that the PI managers align their organizational context with the project management framework. Careful understanding of the strategies, players, and current performance drivers for the organization will dictate specific types of methods, intake or evaluation processes, and other aspects of projects.

What to Look for in a PI Professional?

Recruiting and hiring management engineering types is often difficult. The mix of skills, education, and previous experience is vital. During the formative years, it is important to recruit individuals eager to build and adapt, because the structure and methods will not exist from day 1. Flexibility is a key skill, although it is difficult to measure.

Phase 1	**Phase 2**	**Phase 3**
• Business concept • Service delivery model • Recruit management • Develop vision; proposal • Begin identifying initial projects • Develop departmental standards, objectives, and business processes	• Define or adopt quality methodology • Assemble tool kit of methods • Recruit staff and share team expectations • Training • Begin communication and marketing efforts • Share initial results/gains	• Develop project assessment/intake criteria • Develop project scorecard • Performance management for team members • Further integrate department into institutional processes

Figure 4.2 Approach to developing quality teams.

No PI analyst has the same educational background. While in earlier years an industrial engineering degree would be optimal, given its focus on understanding systems concepts and processes, the vast majority of analysts come with business, nursing, information technology, allied health, or numerous other degrees. There are a number of degree programs that focus on data analysis or health informatics that might be useful. A graduate degree in healthcare management, information systems, or business administration would also provide good training. An undergraduate degree requirement is common in most organizations today for this position.

A previous background in internal or external consulting is also ideal. The ability to understand internal customers (often called user groups), facilitate project meetings and creative sessions, listen to clients, and understand the symptoms of larger problems is required. In short, the following skills are necessary:

- Diagnostic capabilities
- Combination of engineering (technical) and organizational development (soft) skills
- Strong skills and training in data analysis
- Project management
- Experience developing and managing Gantt charts
- Customer service
- Communication
- Knowledge of enterprise information systems, databases, and applications
- Systems modeling

Methodology

One of the critical tasks for an emerging department is to choose the right methodology, as we described in Chapter 3. Among the many choices are

1. Six Sigma (define, measure, analyze, improve, control [DMAIC])
2. Lean (Toyota)
3. Plan–do–check–act (PDCA) cycle
4. Theory of constraints
5. Just in time
6. Total Quality Management or continuous quality improvement

In general, most methodologies are somewhat similar. They differ in their focus and tool kit. For example, Lean encourages a primary focus on eliminating waste, while Six Sigma encourages statistical analysis of processes. It does not matter if you follow a specific approach, or if you blend a combination of methods. What is important is that you adopt a standard approach, incorporate some degree of statistical analysis to model the "behavior" or actions of the process, and then develop consensus around potential ways of improving it. A general process improvement methodology and the primary outputs from each phase are shown in Figure 4.3.

Developing New Projects

Once the PI department gains some maturity, however, management should shift its focus toward developing a portfolio of projects. This is done by working with customers to identify and create demand for services. Case studies of successes in initial projects always help other departments visualize the types of results the department is capable of obtaining.

A "request form" is sometimes used by PI departments to help users request resources. Common elements of the request form include the project's scope, background, and business drivers, as well as deadlines and timelines. The project intake process, defined next, is essential to ensuring that the project helps to increase value and is achievable.

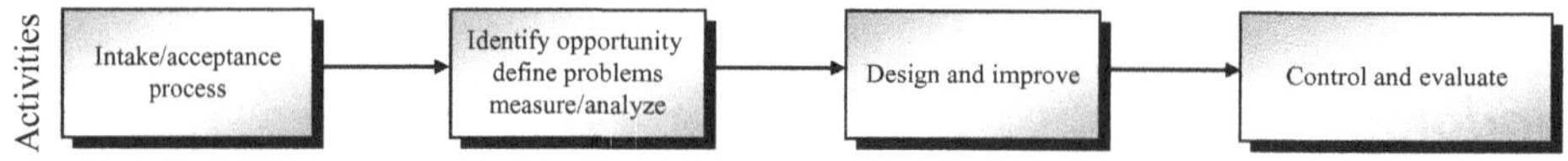

Activities	Intake/acceptance process	Identify opportunity define problems measure/analyze	Design and improve	Control and evaluate
Outputs	Services request	Diagnostic assessment	Proof of concept	Scorecard (metrics)
	Project evaluation model (proposed risk, value, effort matrix)	Process flowcharts (to be, as is)	Training manual	Project summary/closeout
	Project charter	Control charts	Risk/change logs	Case study review
	Project plan	Cause and effect diagrams		
	Budget			

Figure 4.3 Process improvement methodology.

Measuring Project Status

The portfolio of projects underway in large management engineering groups often can be counted in the dozens. Even small groups will have a handful, and understanding and communicating their current status and risk with managers, customers, and other stakeholders can be difficult. Groups should adopt some form of dashboard, to quickly visualize status and alert the reader of the report to any potential problems. One common way to do this is through a frequently updated dashboard or performance scorecard. A performance scorecard is a visual summary of the key performance indicators' status toward goals. Scorecards track each project and then identify key aspects of the project. A sample dashboard, using a "stoplight" approach, is shown in Figure 4.4.

Recommendations on Building Capacity

Capacity refers to the organization's ability to deliver something. Capacity for quality improvement projects is gained when new teams are formed, when methodologies are adopted, and when projects get deployed. There are several recommendations for ensuring that your new PI department is successful.

New Departments Take Time

It is a natural expectation for consultants to hope for immediate results, but in complex organizations, even PI departments take time to cultivate. New initiatives tend to be seen as a disruption to the status quo, or people's area

Project	Analyst	% work complete /total effort	Next major milestone	Schedule/ budget status	Risks
Clinical EMR rollout	Smith	95% 600 days	Seeking CNO approval in may	On track (green)	High (red)
Financial record digitization project	Bobbins	72% 289 days	Mid-February rollout to users	Delayed (yellow)	Medium (yellow)
Supply chain re-design	Moore	3% on hold	Pending upgrades to key ERP system	On hold (red)	High (red)
Modeling and queuing of emergency rooms	Roose	70% 200 days	Presented findings to Dr. Cox	On track	Low (green)

Figure 4.4   Project scorecard or dashboard.

of comfort, and there is almost always resistance to change. We recommend setting expectations for new departments to start slowly—helping to address projects systematically and develop the necessary tools, documentation, and methodology precisely and with rigor.

Train Your PI Professionals

Do not allow PI analysts to work on a project if they are not prepared or trained. However, there is not a comprehensive training program that can help you educate your PI or management engineers. This is often a critical bottle-neck for new departmental rollouts. Projects might also fail if they are staffed by a quality analyst who does not understand the methodologies and tools or lacks facilitation and project management skills. If this happens in the early stages, the fate of the new department is questionable at best. The initial results will dictate how successful the group will be in the long term, since it is nearly impossible to reverse early perceptions from clients and management.

Experience, education, former project experience, and former healthcare training are all important, but they don't really help to teach somebody how to become a better analyst or project professional for PI. While some associations (such as the Healthcare Information and Management Systems Society [HIMSS] or Society for Health Systems) offer educational webinars and tools, you will likely have to develop a custom educational program using a variety of websites, conferences, books, and societies to really jump-start a good PI department.

Avoid Getting Mired in Bureaucracy

Many divisions in large organizations have multiple departments similar to PI or management engineering. It is important to view these as partners, helping to collaboratively achieve results, and not as competitors. Internal competition not only directs your efforts to the wrong areas, but also dis-tracts you from getting critical successes early in the department's develop-ment, educating your staff, and formalizing your methodologies. These are the critical tasks that management must remain focused on.

Learning Organizations

Continuous improvement is really about developing capabilities to con-tinuously learn, adapt, and grow. The knowledge creation that results can change organizational culture and create sustainable value. A *learning organization* is one that improves actions and behaviors through new information that is regularly created and shared (Senge, 2006; Fiol and Lyles, 1985). Garvin (1993) proposed four steps for learning organizations that seem especially well suited for healthcare:

1. Embrace systematic problem solving. Focus on using data and methods to systematically improve decisions and choices.
2. Use experiments and pilots and small change efforts to find new ideas.
3. Learn from the organization's past successes and failures, as well as others.
4. Share, or transfer, that knowledge within the organization to all employees, teams, and departments. Knowledge transfer of the learning is essential to continuous improvement.

One of the things that successful PI departments do is to keep focused on business value, whether it is measured in better clinical quality, cycle time reductions, cost improvements, enhanced internal controls, or any other measurements. Focusing on the real objective of quality management—improving performance—needs to always be at the top of the mind in the early years of formation.

To do this, at both the outset of new projects and the closure of existing ones, needs to be finalized with a formal case study case study or pre- and postproject reviews. These reviews should explore the gaps between initial and final performance indicators of the project. Converting these metrics into value will allow management to share results and gain momentum.

This success, or value, increases the demand for services in the future. The amount of demand for project or PI work is one measure of how well the department is doing internally.

Summary

Managing the PI function is extremely complex. While other functions eventually become routine and operationalized, the job of a management engineer or quality consultant is to constantly be immersed in something new—a new process, a new system, new customers, new departments, and new locations. Understanding the basics of project management structure, which can be adapted and applied in many ways over time, is essential to repeated success. Developing a department or unit to perform PI requires leadership, hiring the right people, adopting good methods, selecting the right projects, and managing for results. The use of Six Sigma tools and methods, especially statistical process control to analyze process behavior and the measurement of defects and process capabilities, represents a great opportunity for healthcare process improvement. Management of all these areas is vital to PI success.

Key Terms

Business concept, capacity, learning organization, performance scorecard

Discussion Questions

1. Why is a business concept important for creating a new quality function?
2. How would you approach management to propose a new department?
3. Which organizations would you choose to benchmark against? How would you find them?
4. Is your organization a learning organization?
5. What elements you would suggest go on an organization's performance scorecard?

References

Fiol CM and Lyles MA (1985). Organizational learning. *Academy of Management Review*, 10(4), 803–813.

Garvin David A (1993). Building a Learning Organization. *Harvard Business Review*. 71(4), July–August 1993, 78–91.

Langabeer J, DelliFraine J, and Helton J (2010). Mixing finance and medicine: The evolution of financial practices in healthcare. *Strategic Finance*, December, 26–34.

Senge P (2006). *Fifth Discipline: The Art and Practice of the Learning Organization.* 2nd edn. New York: Currency/Doubleday Books.

Chapter 5

Project Management

James Langabeer and Rigoberto Delgado

Contents

> Success is not final, failure is not fatal. It is the courage to continue that counts.
>
> **Winston Churchill**
> *Former UK Prime Minister*

Introduction

Projects are undertaken to create value and improve performance. A *project* is an organized effort involving a sequence of activities that are temporarily being performed to achieve a desired outcome. Since they are temporary and involve a variety of individuals and activities, it is important to organize and manage projects appropriately. Similarly, the change that results from projects must be closely managed. This chapter discusses how performance improvement professionals can use project management methods and tools to maximize benefits and minimize the disruptions that change creates.

Project Management

Project management is the application of knowledge, skills, tools, and techniques to project activities to meet the project requirements (Project Management Institute, 2017; PMBOK, 2013). Since all projects have a start and an end, the key to management is to successfully navigate that project through the various stages to ultimate completion and achievement of success. There are three high-level phases in project management, which project managers need to understand well:

1. *Project initiation and design.* This entails the assessment and selection of a new project and its design. This entails all aspects of project planning, which we will describe below.

2. *Project execution.* This entails the control and delivery of the project, including the management of the budget, personnel, schedules, improvement activities, and other aspects of management.

3. *Project closure.* This entails performing all the necessary organizational steps to closing out a project (such as budget and moving personnel back to assigned departments), as well as performing post-project reviews outlining the outcomes and learning opportunities that result from the project.

Each of these will be described below in more detail (Figure 5.1).

Project Initiation and Design

The desired outcome for a project is typically defined as meeting the requirements initially established in the design phase, but it also means ensuring that the project meets a combination of being *on time, on budget, and on scope.* Chapter 4 pointed out, however, that in order to produce real value, it must be aligned with strategic goals, have desirable productivity or performance impacts, and create value. All these outcomes are achievable, but the performance improvement analyst plays a big role in ensuring that the deliverables are met.

Projects move through multiple steps, moving from initial business case justification to project design, analysis, implementation, and post-project reviews. Once the projected has been initiated, the most important aspect is to provide control, or management, to ensure that it progresses as planned to avoid surprises and delays. This aspect of project management is called planning.

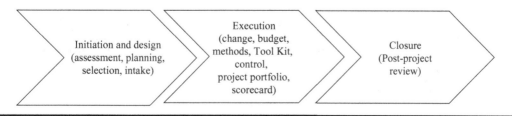

Figure 5.1 Phases in project management.

Project Planning

In many large projects, especially information systems implementations, there might be thousands of activities (or tasks) to be performed by dozens of people (or resources). To track these activities and resources over time, it is necessary to use several tracking mechanisms to predict and monitor progress. A *Gantt chart* is typically used as the project plan in large projects. Figure 5.2 shows a sample visual graphic of a project plan or Gantt chart.

Use of analytical methods such as *program evaluation and review technique* (PERT) and *critical path method* (CPM) are two ways of estimating the most desirable path toward achieving project deliverables (on time, on scope, and under budget). CPM attempts to sequence the activities on the project plan in such a way as to minimize total times, by identifying the longest (or most critical) path and staging all the surrounding tasks around it. PERT uses a simple formula that combines the most optimistic or best-case times (*O*), most pessimistic or worst-case times (*P*), and most likely expected times (*M*) to estimate total project duration. The formula is expressed as the sum of the optimistic (*O*) and pessimistic (*P*) times,

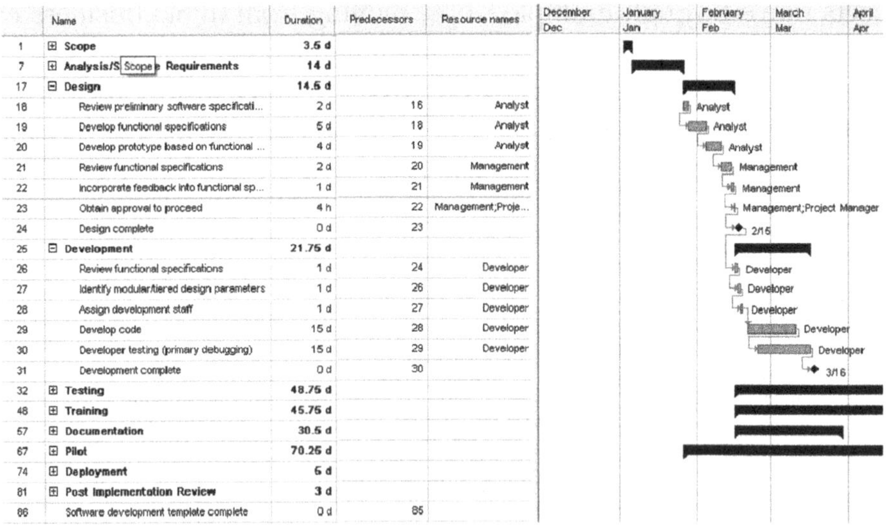

Figure 5.2   Project plan or Gantt chart.

plus 4 times the most likely (*M*) divided by 6. Mathematically, this is expressed as

$$\text{PERT} = [O + P + 4M] \div 6$$

So, if a project should most likely require 10 working days, but in the worst case could take 20 days, and if everything was ideal could be completed in 5 days, then PERT would suggest that the engineer should use 10.83 days as the expected project duration. This is a very valuable technique for estimating projects, but it must be based on thorough examination of all details in the project plan.

In most cases, the project's start date is assigned based on funding or approval timing. The end date, or project completion date, is usually determined in one of three ways:

1. Sometimes it is given as a "mandate," due to executive order, legal or regulatory timelines, or other constraints.
2. It could be computed mathematically through a bottom-up approach, using PERT or CPM as described above, to add up all project tasks and realistically determine timelines.
3. A top-down "rough-cut" planning process can be used where key activities are discussed and critical paths are explored for these high-level events.

Once a project has defined these two dates, the project plan is essentially one of breaking down tasks into specific functions by responsible party. It depends on the amount of resources (personnel, time, and finances) in total and by component. This is sometimes referred to as *work breakdown structure* (WBS).

When planning projects, it is advisable to describe the purpose and intent of a project. A *project charter* describes the project's purpose, plans, assumptions, and roles. This document helps to lay the foundation for how a project will be organized. An example is provided in the form (sample project charter) shown below.

Sample Project Charter

Project Name: _____
Division: _____
Product/Process: _____
Prepared by: _____
Version Control #: _____

PROJECT CHARTER PURPOSE

Describe the strategic charter or purpose of the project.

PROJECT EXECUTIVE SUMMARY

Summarize the key points of each of the following: Business requirements, Scope, Goals, objectives, estimates, work plan, budget, and overall approach

PROJECT JUSTIFICATION

Briefly describe the rationale and business justification for undertaking this project.

PROJECT SCOPE

Goals and Objectives

Goals	Objectives
1.	
2.	

Organizational Impacts

Organization	Estimated Impact

Project Deliverables

Milestone	Deliverable
1. Milestone Description	• Deliverable 1—description • Deliverable 2—description • Deliverable n—description
2. Milestone Description	• Deliverable 1—description • Deliverable 2—description

Deliverables Out of Scope

List anything that is out of scope or that the project will explicitly consider

Project Estimated Costs & Duration

Project Key Milestone	Date Estimated	Deliverable(s) Included	Confidence Level
Milestone 1		Deliverable 1 Deliverable 2	High/Medium/Low
Milestone 2		Deliverable 1	High/Medium/Low

PROJECT CRITERIA

Project Assumptions

- Assumption 1
- Assumption 2
- Assumption 3

Forecasted Project Issues:

Priority Criteria

- High-priority issue impacting critical path. Immediate resolution required.

- Medium-priority issue, requiring mitigation before next milestone.

- Low-priority issue, and can be resolved prior to project completion.

#	Date	Priority	Owner	Description	Status & Resolution
1				Issue 1 description	Resolution
2				Issue 2 description	Resolution

Forecasted Project Risks

#	Risk Area	Likelihood	Owner	Project Impact Mitigation Plan
1	Project Risk	H, M, L		Mitigation Plan
2				

Project Constraints

- Constraint 1

- Constraint 2

Project Team Organization Plans

Project Team Role	Project Team Member	Responsibilities
Role, Title		

APPROVALS

_____   _____

Project Manager   Executive Sponsor

_____

Organizing Projects

Since the project planning involves dividing up tasks by role, it is usually necessary to include a project organization chart that clarifies roles, responsibilities, and parties involved in the process dedicated to the specific project. For example, assume the sponsor of a particular project is the hospital's chief executive officer, is led by a project manager from the management engineering department, and has leads from a number of areas. Figure 5.3 shows a sample project organization chart for this project.

Since projects typically are ad hoc and temporary, they most often involve matrix organizational structures, where daily operational reporting roles are clearly delineated or superimposed by the project structure. Such matrix organizations are very common in healthcare projects today.

Project Identification and Selection

Projects are often assigned to quality or performance improvement managers from someone else in the organization, but many times they are identified and selected based on criteria. For instance, a hospital with continuous

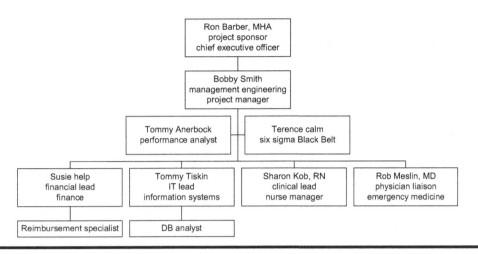

Figure 5.3   Project organization chart.

issues in managing infection rates might identify a project to measure and mitigate these rates to improve the safety of the organization. In this case, project identification, assessment, and selection are of critical importance.

One of the critical steps in managing a process improvement function is to closely examine how projects are selected. Given constraints in financial and human resources, as all organizations have, it is critical to have a project intake, or acceptance process, that selects projects that are of high strategic value, and optimize given resources.

Quality improvement projects tend to encompass multiple functions, disciplines, and operational areas within a hospital. In this respect, management engineers often face challenges of supporting multiple end-user groups with conflicting objectives and resource needs. Proper allocation of resources should be done considering three key factors: financial impact (F) related to economic value generated by the organization; productivity impact and operational performance (P) involving the effect on human and physical resources; and strategic alignment (A), measured by how well a project complies with the hospital's strategy. These dimensions, which we call the FPA space, summarize the relevant business drivers and provide a framework for the justification, implementation, and long-term evaluation of new initiatives. Ideally, if an organization could select a project that was high in the FPA space, then it would maximize outcomes. Understanding how to incorporate the FPA space concept into a project development process, however, can be challenging and frustrating. Here we present a framework to be used in the delivery and assessment of effective management engineering projects.

Risk, however, impacts the potential value of any new project. We explore this first, before discussing a method for incorporating risk into project assessment.

Project Risks

Risk is an uncertainty that could negatively impact project outcomes. Risks are positively correlated with the need for strong project management: the greater the risks, the greater the need for skilled facilitation, control, and management. Risks may take many forms. One major risk is long project times. As projects stretch out into multiple quarters and years, they are more likely to encounter staff turnover, funding or other resource shifting, and lower degrees of focus and momentum in later periods. Larger-scale and larger-scope projects also bring higher risks. Implementation of large electronic medical records in multiple hospitals, for example, involves wide scale and scope, and is always complex. Cross-functional, multidepartmental projects are also high risk, as they stretch boundaries. Other common risks include lack of training, poor communication, lack of funding, organizational politics, and inadequate preparation on the part of the engineer or analyst. All these can be avoided by managing risks.

There are many performance improvement analysts that worry more about potential risks than about ensuring that deliverables and positive outcomes are generated. Although it is vital to identify and mitigate risks wherever possible, it is important to not let risks prevent project success. At a minimum, this entails documenting risks as they are discovered, logging them into the project database or files, sharing them with the project team and sponsors, and identifying contingency plans in the event that the risk materializes. A risk issues log helps control risks and ensure that mitigation plans are in place for all identified risks.

Figure 5.4 shows a summary of a risk issues log used in successful quality improvement projects.

The ultimate result is to present an objective approach to review and justify a project proposal. We start by reexamining *net present value* (NPV) approach for the selection of a project, followed by other approaches to valuing a project's impact in the organization.

RISK MANAGEMENT LOG			
Project: Surgery dept. capacity analysis **Analyst:** Michelle Moore			**Date:** 03/29/2018
Date risk identified	**Risk type**	**Detail/impact**	**Severity**
02/05/18	Financial	Budget reduced by $50,000; system acquisition not likely	Low
03/01/18	Personnel	Lopez reassigned out of project; could delay timeline 6 weeks	High
03/17/18	Scope	Sponsor added 2 new goals	Low
03/21/18	Technical	Integration with ERP system poorly defined	Medium
03/23/18	Organizational	Merger underway with new hospital; could impact project priority	High

Figure 5.4   Risk issues log. ERP, enterprise resource planning.

Incorporating Risk in Project Selection

Project outcomes include improvement in clinical safety, a reduction in the variability of a process, or better patient satisfaction. Sometimes, however, the impact can be financial or economic. Reduction of non-value-added steps or streamlined process flows often results in fewer resource utilization. In this case, a good tool to understand is the concept of NPV. NPV is a method for converting future cash inflows (benefits) and outflows (expenditures) into a single value in today's terms, to evaluate whether a project makes financial sense.

An information technology (IT) project, like any other investment, does not have guaranteed returns or payoffs. Several levels of returns, or even losses, may take place in the future, and this uncertainty is what defines a project's risk level. Since payoffs vary by project, however, how is it possible to compare different projects? A common approach is NPV, which, as seen in the formula below, discounts a project's present and future costs and benefits by using the project's risk level as a component of the discount factor.

$$\text{NPV}_i = \sum{}^{t} \left(B_t - C_t \right) \big/ \left(1 - r \right)^t$$

The r in the formula is the risk level specific to the project. Several factors, such as demand for the products and technology, determine the level of risk involved with a specific project; however, at the institutional level the following criteria can be used to define a project's risk level:

■ Length of time required to implement the project
■ Existing skills and experience in implementing similar projects
■ Technical complexity involved in the implementation
■ End-user and management level of support for the project
■ Magnitude of the change brought about with the project

Considering all these factors and summarizing them into a single measurement of risk is extremely difficult. A practical approach is to make a subjective assessment involving a group of individuals not involved in the project. The group is asked to assign projects, based on the specified criteria, into one of three categories: low risk, medium risk, and high risk. Once the projects have been assigned, the NPV can be calculated for each project using the ranges of r levels, as shown in Table 5.1. Note that the ranges can be customized based on what is acceptable in your own organization.

Table 5.2 shows an example of two projects' cash flows with varying levels of risk.

Depending on the useful project life, the analysis is normally done considering a five-year period. Rather than obtaining a single value for NPV,

Table 5.1 Risk Levels

Risk Level	r Range (%)
Low	5
Medium	5–10
High	20

Table 5.2 Project Comparison (in thousands of dollars)

* in $,000		FY1	FY2	FY3	FY4	FY5	Total
Project 1	Expected revenue	$0	$50	$75	$100	$150	
	Costs	$290	$0	$0	$0	$0	
	Benefits	($290)	$50	$75	$100	$150	$85
Project 2	Expected revenue	$0	$150	$125	$50	$25	
	Costs	$290					
	Benefits	($290)	$150	$125	$50	$25	$60

it is preferable to provide a range of NPV values, which allows managers more room for decision making. In this case, Project 1 appears to be less attractive than Project 2. If both projects are considered low risk, Project 1 would be preferred over Project 2. However, if both projects are considered of medium risk, then Project 2 would be preferable over Project 1. Finally, if both projects are considered high risk, neither project should be implemented. Table 5.3 summarizes the analysis incorporating risks.

Measuring Expected Productivity Impact

One item that is rarely considered in project source allocation is measuring the expected impact on productivity and human resources. A simple approach to decompose changes resulting from new technology is ratio comparison, which has been used for analysis in cost changes and expenditures.

Using the following model, we can decompose changes in total production into changes in productivity or personnel:

$$\text{Change in Total Productivity} = I_2 \times (P_2 - P_1) + P_1 \times (I_2 - I_1)$$

where I_i is the level of Full Time Equivalent (FTE) for the ith period and P_i is the level of productivity per FTE for the ith period.

Thus, in a case of two projects showing exactly the same level of potential production as seen in Table 5.4, the cause of change can be different.

Table 5.3 Project Comparison with Risk Analyses

		Low Risk		Medium Risk		High Risk	
Project 1	Risk rate	3%	5%	6%	10%	11%	15%
	Discounted factor $(1+r)$	1.03	1.05	1.06	1.10	1.11	1.15
	Net present value	$52,452	$33,748	$25,184	($4,526)	($10,950)	($33,301)
Project 2	Risk rate	3%	5%	6%	10%	11%	15%
	Discounted factor $(1+r)$	1.03	1.05	1.06	1.10	1.11	1.15
	Net present value	$40,218	$28,567	$23,153	$3,919	($346)	($15,546)

Table 5.4   Project Comparison with Production Changes

	Productivity	*Project 1*	*Project 2*
Current	Current FTEs	10	15
	Current productivity per FTE	3	2
	Total production	30	30
Expected	Future FTEs	9	12
	Future productivity per FTE	4	3
	Total production	36	36
Total change due to productivity changes		9	12
Total change due to FTE changes		−3	−6
Total production change		2	6

The table shows that Project 2 has the advantage of larger changes in production due to productivity improvements. However, this improvement comes as the result of large decreases in labor. If the objective of the institution is to reduce personnel, this project would be acceptable, but if there are concerns of reassigning employees (a condition common in non-for-profit hospitals), Project 1 would be more acceptable. Likewise, projects that impact large increments in productivity can be an objective even at the sacrifice of FTEs. This latter approach can be implemented in cases where there are opportunities to allocate displaced FTEs in high-value activities.

Evaluating a Project's Strategic Alignment

An assessment of a project's potential is not complete without an idea of how it meets the strategic goals of the organization. *Project strategic alignment* is an approach to measuring the degree of similarity between a project and the organization's priorities. It often involves the use of a score or index. One concept that has been discussed is using a system of four factors to determine the outcome of any transformation initiative: *duration, integrity, commitment,* and *effort* (DICE) (Sirkin et al., 2005). Based on scores for each area, it would be possible to predict potential outcomes.

There are several components in establishing a score of a new project: (1) perceived alignment with institutional strategic goals and organizational outcomes, (2) support from senior management, and (3) acceptance on the part of end users. We developed an approach to predicting the impact for a project, using five total factors. As shown in Table 5.5, the score for each category can take a value ranging from 1 to 4, where the lowest value represents a high contribution to the success of the project and the highest value represents the least favorable conditions for success of the project. Applying the formula presented in the table, the best overall score for a project can be a 7, while the worst possible is 28, using the weights assigned in the table.

Based on a scaling system such as this, it is possible to define the strategic importance of any project. For example, a project with a score of less than 14 would be considered of significant strategic importance to the institution, while those scoring 14–20 are less important from the institution's strategic point of view.

Providing a Final Score for the Project

The final assessments include the multifactor description and ranking of the best projects. The overall result is a list of projects ordered in a queue, and the queue is formed from the consideration of the items described above.

A summary of ranking for two illustrative cases is given in Table 5.6.

Table 5.5   Strategic Alignment Factors

Factors for Defining Project Strategic Alignment	Points (1–4)
Impact on organizational outcomes (e.g., market share and patient satisfaction) (X_1)	1
Potential for performance improvement (X_2)	2
Project integration: Alignment with current projects (X_3)	1
Executive sponsorship and commitment (X_4)	2
Customer/end-user commitment (X_5)	2
Weighted score = $X_1 + (2 \times X_2) + (2 \times X_3) + X_4 + X_5$ =	11

Table 5.6   Project Evaluation Summary

Evaluation Type	Project 1	Project 2
Financial/NPV	Medium	Low
Productivity impact	Low	High
Strategic alignment	Medium	High

Transforming each level into numeric values (low = 1, medium = 2, and high = 3) gives us a comparative measure for the two projects, as shown in Figure 5.5. Ideally, where demand for multiple projects exists, organizations should choose one that maximizes all three areas. Figure 5.5 shows a "radar diagram" with the FPA space (financial, performance, and alignment) and a comparison of two projects, where Project 1 ranks higher on strategic alignment and financial outcomes, and Project 2 is stronger on productivity impacts. Based on this summary diagram, Project 1 would appear to maximize alignment, performance, and financials.

Based on these analyses, a project will have to be selected that maximizes the potential results incorporating risks.

Project Execution and Control

During these phases, multiple activities are occurring. This includes managing the team and personnel assigned to the projects; managing the deliverables, timelines, and budget; managing the communication of project performance to the organization; and performing all the necessary process improvement and implementation steps necessary to meet the project requirements.

The Gantt chart shown earlier and a budget-to-actual comparison of resource expenditures in the project are two simple tools to ensure that

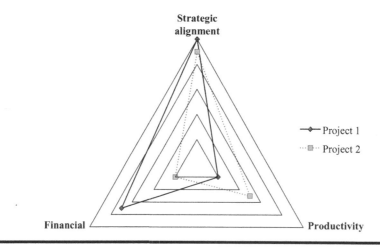

Figure 5.5 Evaluation of project alignment.

project outcomes are on track. Remember that ideally projects should be on time, on budget, and on scope.

Expectations for the Project Team

When projects are initiated, clear communication with all project members must be initiated to set ground rules for behavior and expectations. These expectations can be defined formally, in service level agreements between the project manager and the individual, or they can be generic for the entire team. These expectations include

- Understanding attendance expectations and frequency of project meetings
- Expectations for getting things done within meetings
- Commitment levels, both in team meetings and when members are back in their operational roles
- Confidentiality
- Openness and candor during brainstorming sessions
- Roles in projects, such as meeting "timekeeper," facilitator, recorder, and "parking lot" attendant for notes and ideas
- Knowing how to deal with conflict resolution

Keeping the project team focused on outcomes and progress is one way to ensure that teams do not become mired in bureaucracy or focused on negative tasks. Reviewing project dashboards and focusing on a strategic project framework is one way to ensure focus. A strategic project framework is a simple, one-page summary of the key project objectives, activities, metrics, and goals. A sample framework for one project, conducted for a large hospital supply chain and materials management department, is shown in Figure 5.6.

Change Management

Process improvement efforts result in change—change to individuals and the organization as a whole. While change might be beneficial in the long run, in the near term it creates ambiguity, confusion, and tension if not managed appropriately. *Change management* is a structured attempt to identify and

Project objectives	Become seamless	Automate processes	Financially effective	Retain and recruit talent
Operational activities	• Attend nursing and clinical meetings • Create service level agreements with customers • Partner with vendors • Update policy and procedures manual • Forecasting inventory	• Warehouse scanning solution • Business intelligence reporting	• Establish consignment inventory programs where possible	• Identify current skill sets of employees • Determine skill sets necessary for future roles • Include employee input on policies and procedures
Key performance indicators	• Improved communication with customers • Reduced inventory risk • Improved vendor relationships • Improved efficiencies • Reduced stock-outs	• Improved productivity • Better reporting to analyze costs, improve compliance, and drive standardization	• Improved inventory utilization • Reduced days inventory on hand	• Implement quarterly employee survey • Reduced loss of personnel to other departments
Goals	• Reduction in complaints >10% • Reduction in stock outs by 20%	• Decreased data entry time for requisitions >10% • Reduction in data entry errors >10%	• Inventory value for both warehouses $500,00 0 • Decreased days inventory on hand >5 days	• Ensure each employee receives 24 hours of training per year

Figure 5.6 Strategic project framework.

manage adjustments that will impact the project and operations throughout the organization. Change management aims to improve user acceptance of the change (Cameron and Green, 2004).

The key responsibilities in change management are to

■ Ensure user acceptance and adoption of process changes or technology
■ Identify potential risks and points of resistance for proposed changes, and develop plans to mitigate (or minimize) the disruption of the changes
■ Develop readiness assessment for changes, by examining workflows and personnel impacted
■ Ensure positive acceptance of changes, through communication and relationship development
■ Develop corrective actions to ensure that changes are effective

Performance improvement professionals need to develop a change management plan for each project to minimize disruptions and ensure that the improvements stabilize and remain over time, during the *control* phase of the project. The overall purpose of the change plan is to implement ways of amplifying the project's driving forces and shrinking the resistance forces. The elements of each phase are outlined below.

Create the Conditions for Change

The first step in creating the conditions for change is to communicate the gap between the current state and the end state. This requires securing buy-in from sponsors and support from the top. This is an important component of the communication strategy, as it relates the key players in the change process. Communicate change to all those affected. Also, you should identify potential opposition and contact potential sponsors.

Next, it is important to create a sense of urgency. This will be accomplished by presenting demonstrations on new technology emphasizing the benefits of making the change: shorter cycle, paperless, and higher security and efficiency.

Finally, all must agree on a change plan and timeline for achieving the end state. At the end of the testing cycle, the management engineer or project manager will conduct an evaluation of deliverables and will secure approval from management to proceed with full-scale deployment of the project.

Make Change Happen

There are four key activities to make change occur:

1. Develop awareness, communication, and training programs tailored to each target group. All the users who will be impacted, as well other stakeholders, need to be prepared in advance for the changes that will occur.
2. Create and communicate the vision. This is a critical element in guiding the change effort. The key factor, however, is to provide an "actionable" mission, a concise statement that articulates the purpose of the new process, system, or solution. For example, a vision for a new patient kiosk in a clinic might be to "make patient registration fast and easy."
3. Form an advisory or empowerment team. The team will consist of no more than four advisors representing different user segments. Regular meetings with the advisory team should improve communication, help identify and eliminate bottlenecks, and handle resistance.
4. Publicize the transformation target date. This is the date when the new process will replace an existing process. Understanding timelines and dates helps impacted users understand the changes coming.

Make Change Permanent

Once you have created the conditions for change, and successfully made the change, then it becomes important to make it permanent, or "sticky." This means to remain in place once the project team disbands and returns back to their original positions. This is not as easy as one might expect.

One of the first guidelines for making change stick is to maintain the empowering structures for a period of time post-project. The objective is to open channels of communication with the end-user community and includes two basic activities. Retaining the advisory team for 6 months after the new process or solution go-live date is a good idea. If a "help desk" is used for the transition (e.g., in the case of a large system migration or implementation), the help desk could analyze call patterns and periodically make proactive calls to users to ensure usage and understanding of the new solution. If comment or suggestion boxes are used, they can help to gather ideas and to keep the user community involved and active in the process.

It is also necessary to identify and minimize barriers to change. Removing structures that hinder the optimal functioning of the new process is a critical step in the success of the project. Identifying barriers will result from the work of the advisory team and feedback from the help desk. Removing those barriers, however, will involve interactions with management.

Organizations also might consider implementing financial incentives. Individuals involved in implementing new projects should receive financial rewards based on the goals of the project and clear key performance indicator objectives.

Lastly, making change stick involves measuring and communicating the value (e.g., economic, cycle time, and patient satisfaction) gained with the new process or system (Rye, 2001). The impact assessment is the final phase of the project management process, and its goal is to provide management with objective data on the benefits of the new solution and to gain support for follow-up projects. The results of the assessment should be shared with end users to improve acceptance and encourage further improvement.

Roles in the Change Process

Selecting a list of individuals to carry out the different tasks of communication and promotion allows project managers to increase the potential for success. There are four broad roles:

1. Sponsors (people who legitimize and authorize the change)
2. Change agents (individuals who are tasked with planning and executing the change)
3. Advocates (those who request and support the change)
4. Targets (individuals who will have to live with the change, such as end users)

Each of these types has a role to play in the change process and ultimately helps to determine project outcomes.

Project Communication

Communication is vital to managing change (Ristino, 2000). Two components of communication plans are the strategy and "brand positioning." The communication strategy outlines the channels of communication, while the brand position statements define the message (content and direction).

Given its level of use among the target groups, e-mail is almost always an important component of the communication strategy. Communication frequency needs to be outlined as well. The greater the change, the more frequently the communication should occur. A strategy may include other elements, as shown in Table 5.7.

In addition to the communication strategy, brand positioning needs to be outlined. This includes identification of the following.

Customer Need and Benefits

State what the need is for the customer or the benefits to the user group. If the process has a definite impact on the users, this should be amplified in all communication prior to the new process going live. Time savings,

Table 5.7   Communication Channels

Channel	Suggested Frequency (Example)	Action
Mass e-mail	Product release	Targeted mass mail-out
Employee forums	As needed	Article describing new process or solution
Newsletter	Quarterly	Article describing the new solution
New employee orientation	As needed	Materials for the orientation packet

elimination of manual entry, and reduction in rework are all great benefits for customers. Brand positioning statements in communication should reinforce this. For example, "the new process will eliminate the need for you to make three copies of all invoices."

Brand Character

The new process should be characterized by communication that reflects the character or personality of the new process or solution. For example, if a new automated system for patient registration was implemented, such as a self-service kiosk, the communication might use terms such as *effective*, *painless*, and *secure*. Words play a very important part in the mind-set and perception that will ultimately become reality.

Project Management Office

In certain instances, management engineers have helped to create a *project management office* (PMO). A PMO is a group of professionals that assist management in developing structure and standards for more sophisticated management of projects (Englund et al., 2003). Typically, PMOs are created to assist in the deployment of IT, and report to the chief information officer, although in reality PMOs can be used for any type of organizational project. Since most large systems have literally dozens of large projects, and hundreds of smaller IT projects, in the portfolio, a PMO functions as the portfolio manager to some degree—ensuring that risks are being mitigated and that a comprehensive view of all projects is available for the chief information officer and other executives in the governance process.

The PMO has two primary roles:

1. Developing standards for governance (evaluation, planning, management, and control) of projects, and ensuring that these standards are being followed across the organization consistently
2. Managing the organizational perspective of IT, which primarily involves institutional project portfolio management

Portfolio management is a term being used widely in IT lately, but it was "borrowed" from the financial sector, where financial portfolios are common. Although it has many definitions, portfolio management is defined here as the systematic governance of projects with an aim toward maximizing value or utility across the organization, while managing risks.

With its focus on value creation, PMOs have to take the lead in ensuring that all projects have defined performance expectations—benefits are clearly documented in the project evaluation stages, and then on an ongoing basis both during the project and postimplementation. Since many benefits are often left ambiguous (many times on purpose by project managers), PMOs have to consistently require and enforce quantitative expressions of benefits wherever possible as part of the governance processes. Management of the portfolio requires having a complete perspective on performance contributions by project.

Because of their skill sets, management engineers and performance improvement analysts are often selected to staff, consult, or lead in PMO creation and management. Their expertise in metrics and methods helps to ensure that the standards set are realistic and routinely applied to all projects. The development of accurate performance metrics is probably one of the biggest opportunity areas.

PMOs should be evaluated by their "reach" across the organization, and for the project success rates—essentially defined as the percentage of projects that both reach the desired milestones on time, on budget, and on scope, and achieve the deliverables (i.e., performance benefits) expressed in the governance process. To do this, the PMOs need to develop a collaborative consulting approach where PMO analysts reach out to the organization and continuously offer advice and assistance. Sometimes, this might be tactical assistance in understanding documentation and methodologies, or be might be more strategic assistance in resolving project issues and hitches. Given the focus of PMOs to help standardize processes, it is a clear risk or danger to avoid taking a "command and control" approach, where mandates and a centralized approach to projects exist. This approach is destined to fail. PMOs should instead focus on developing a service-line approach. As such, PMOs services should offer

■ Training of project professionals throughout the organization
■ Development and deployment of standards, methodologies, and documentation
■ Routine communication newsletters and updates, to keep project managers engaged at a more strategic level
■ Definition of, and keeping visibility on, key performance indicators for key processes across the organization
■ Evaluation, acquisition, and training around project software and tools

Summary

Managing projects is a learned skill. Organizing resources and activities logically and efficiently produces more optimal results. Techniques such as CPM and PERT help to design optimal sequencing of the project plan. Risk should be actively incorporated into all phases, from project selection to control. Risks should also be identified and mitigated. Projects force change, however, and the principles and mechanisms for managing change should be incorporated into all projects. Communication strategies with brand positioning should be included on a regular basis in all communication with organizational stakeholders in order to prepare and accept changes.

Key Terms

Change management, charter, critical path method (CPM), Gantt chart, Monte Carlo simulation, net present value, on budget, on scope, on time, portfolio management, project management office, project strategic alignment, program evaluation and risk technique (PERT), risk, work breakdown structure

Discussion Questions

1. How should you decide which project to take on in your organization? How do you set those priorities?
2. Which method is best to use to estimate an optimal project path?
3. How should risk be identified during a project, and what are the most important risks you could envision?
4. How is change management a useful skill for quality analysts?

References

Cameron E and Green M (2004). *Making Sense of Change Management: A Complete Guide to the Models, Tools & Techniques of Organizational Change*. London: Kogan Page.

Englund RL, Graham RJ, and Dinsmore PC (2003). *Creating the Project Office: A Manager's Guide to Leading Organizational Change*. New York: Wiley.

Lewis JP (2006). *Fundamentals of Project Management*. New York: AMACOM.

PMBOK (2013). *A Guide to the Project Management Body of Knowledge (PMBOK Guide)*. 5th edn. Newtown Square, PA: Project Management Institute.

Project Management Institute (2017). What is project management? Available at www.PMI.org.

Ristino RJ (2000). *The Agile Manager's Guide to Managing Change*. Bristol, VT: Velocity Business Publishing.

Rye C (2001). *Change Management: The 5-Step Action Kit*. London: Kogan Page.

Sirkin HL, Keenan P, and Jackson A (2005). The hard side of change management. *Harvard Business Review*, 83(10) October 2005, 109–118 109–118.

Chapter 6

Process Redesign

Kim Brant-Lucich

Contents

Simplicity is the ultimate sophistication.

Leonardo da Vinci
Inventor

Introduction

As we discussed in Chapter 1, the term *process improvement* is frequently used synonymously with *performance improvement, process redesign,* and *business process reengineering.* All seek to simplify processes to improve outputs and enhance value or achieve excellence. In this chapter, process redesign will focus on enhancing the tasks and activities involved in transforming an input into an output.

Process Redesign

In the case of most processes, *better* suggests greater efficiency and/or effectiveness—a more expedient process, fewer errors, minimal redundancy, and reduced waste. In this chapter, we focus on several scenarios in process redesign. Recall that a *process* is a set of linked activities and tasks that are performed in sequence to achieve a specific goal or produce a deliverable or output. *Process redesign* is redesigning a process to streamline, simplify, and enhance value. Process redesign can utilize multiple methods (e.g., Lean, which focuses on maximizing value-added activities, or Kanban [small, continuous improvements]).

The first scenario we will describe involves improving a medical office physician charting process. Figure 6.1 is a high-level conceptual depiction of a process as something that is triggered by an event or action, and which then transforms inputs into outputs. The text at the bottom of the picture provides an example of a sample process for medical office charting.

An acting teacher of mine always used to say, "It doesn't matter how you get there, as long as you get there." At a macrolevel, the same could be said of process improvement, although it would be naïve, and likely very costly, to assume that "anything goes" or that a methodology is not required. The challenge is to determine what approach is right for your organization, optimal timelines, and resource constraints of the

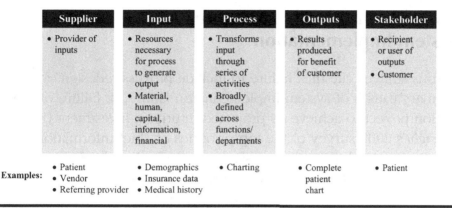

Supplier	Input	Process	Outputs	Stakeholder
• Provider of inputs	• Resources necessary for process to generate output • Material, human, capital, information, financial	• Transforms input through series of activities • Broadly defined across functions/ departments	• Results produced for benefit of customer	• Recipient or user of outputs • Customer

	Supplier	Input	Process	Outputs	Stakeholder
Examples:	• Patient • Vendor • Referring provider	• Demographics • Insurance data • Medical history	• Charting	• Complete patient chart	• Patient

Figure 6.1   Physician office charting process.

implementation. Approaches vary from simple process improvement driven by process modeling and analysis to technology-driven process simulation to Lean Six Sigma. The point of my acting teacher's direction was to steer actors away from overthinking the means of getting to the desired outcome, and instead focus on the result. The result, in the case of a process improvement, would be a process that is better than it was before the system implementation project began. The same acting teacher used to always say, "No one wants to see your homework." That may not be true of all teachers, though!

With regards to process improvement, most senior executives do not want to see all details in a process—rather, they want a high-level (summary) picture of challenges, improvement opportunities, and results. Management communications and reporting, however, are worthy of a book chapter of their own. Suffice it to say that management communications should always be concise and to the point, but inclusive enough to provide an accurate picture of the situation. The purpose of this chapter is to demystify the art of process improvement. Process improvement can be thought of as an art rather than a science because, although it requires analysis and logic, a certain degree of creativity and intuition is desirable. In addition, since people are involved in most processes, knowledge and understanding of human nature and organizational culture is also an integral component of process improvement. This chapter provides an applied overview to process redesign, and outlines a very basic, reusable methodology that can be integrated with system implementation to improve the likelihood of project success and user adoption.

Importance of Process Improvement in System Implementation

Numerous sources cite the "failure to include process redesign" as one of the primary causes of system implementation failure, or failure of the implementation project to achieve its projected return on investment (ROI). In *CIO Insight*'s 2008 survey of the top priorities of chief information officers (CIOs), "improving business processes" was ranked as the second-highest priority, right behind improving customer service (Alter, 2007). Moving forward to 2017, numerous sources indicate that CIOs have shifted their thinking, placing high priority on strategic alignment, as well as on innovation and disruption. This certainly doesn't mean that process improvement is no longer important. It does, however, highlight the idea that system implementation should be used as an opportunity to be both disruptive and innovative in addressing the processes that are supported by the system to be implemented (Chang, 2017). Typically, when budgets are being reviewed for project approval, the first thing to be eliminated is the line item for "process analyst" or "change manager." When I worked as a consultant, I saw clients balk at spending money on process improvement or change management. They merely wanted to "get the system in" as quickly and inexpensively as possible and didn't think that the resources required to analyze, document, and improve processes as part of implementation were necessary.

This was so often the case that consultants disparagingly referred to it as "system slamming," or slamming in the system with no regard for the people or processes affected. Often, there is the assumption that processes can be revisited and refined once the system is in place. Organizations view process work as unnecessary, and often trade the individuals performing that function for the more technical skills of software development, interface development, testing, system training, and project management. Often, the project manager is expected to "manage change," which includes any changes to processes, policies, and procedures. A good project manager may have the ability to manage the system implementation life cycle, as well as managing people, issues, and risks. But if process improvement is not an integral and mandatory line item on a work plan, it is likely to be overlooked. Typically, a project manager might identify the need for process work, but the organization (or client) pushes back and claims that there isn't time for "a bunch of people to sit around doing process flows that will only end up in a notebook and never get looked at again."

The fact is that process flows do often end up in notebooks, which eventually become dusty. However, if a process is not assessed or improved prior to defining system requirements, then the requirements will be based on existing processes, and the system implementation will be nothing more than automation of the existing, and often poorly designed, process. The system, once implemented, may seem to add additional burdensome extra steps to the existing process, so users will find work-arounds to avoid using the system, and adoption will be low. When adoption is poor, there is little to no ROI for the investment in information technology. It is at this point that organizations generally bring in a team after the fact to "fix" the implementation.

Today, more hospitals, health systems, and physician offices are moving toward common electronic medical record (EMR) systems, with up to 50% of hospitals using a common EMR. These providers typically expect that the system itself will solve all its problems. Many of these implementations have process improvement built into the system design, as the system was developed and modified over many years, based on the clinical workflows it supports. In these cases, workflow training is a key element of the implementation. This is an example of the system implementation driving the process change and not the process improvement driving the system design.

Basic Process Improvement Approach

There are a variety of process improvement methodologies that can be applied to system implementation. Lean Six Sigma has become the latest trend in the healthcare industry since about 2002, with numerous health organizations jumping on the bandwagon, and a host of conferences and seminars dedicated to applying Toyota's Lean Production System to healthcare. However, prior to the push for Lean Six Sigma, the standard approach was what I like to refer to as the "old-fashioned method" of process improvement. This involves a few basic steps, not unlike the Lean approach:

1. Documentation and evaluation of existing processes (referred to as "current state" or "as is" process), and identification of risks and improvement opportunities. *Current state* is a representation of a process as it currently exists, prior to any changes.
2. Visioning or design of the future state, or "to be" process. *Future state* is a representation of the desired end state for a process, which should have higher value and is more streamlined.

3. Conducting gap analysis. *Gaps* are the difference between the current and future states.
4. Implementing a plan for getting from the current state to the future state.

To be truly comprehensive, all four steps should consider people, process, and technology—people performing a process step, the process itself, and any enabling technology that supports (or does not support) the current or future state process. The gap analysis and implementation plans should address what needs to take place to bridge the gaps, for example, communication and training, technology requirements, and workflow redesign. These steps may seem like an oversimplification of the process, but in my experience, these are critical to beginning a process redesign effort and, more specifically, critical to system implementation. The four basic steps must be completed before the process improvement can begin and before system development efforts start. Within those steps, there are varying degrees of rigor that may be applied, from root cause analysis to computerized process simulation, depending on the need, skill set of staff, and availability of simulation tools.

Lean Six Sigma

As we discussed earlier, the Lean Six Sigma approach to process improvement is similar in theory to the process described above, although the tools and methods differ, and a greater degree of rigor is applied to identifying and eliminating process waste (Lean) and reducing process variation (Six Sigma). Lean is a facilitative approach, engaging multiple users, documenting standard work, using process simulation (not computerized) to facilitate the brainstorming of improvements, conducting experiments, and observing and timing processes. Statistical tools may also be applied, which is where the Six Sigma component of Lean enters the picture. For an organization to use Lean as its standard approach to process improvement, Lean must be identified as an organizational strategy, and must be embedded in the corporate culture. Using Lean requires strong senior leadership support and a well-trained staff with the skill sets required to facilitate Lean process improvement. It would be extremely naive to decide to use Lean Six Sigma for one system implementation if it is not the methodology currently in place across the enterprise, as success requires culture change. There are, however, many Lean tools that may be incorporated into old-fashioned process improvement, if team members are trained and skilled in the use of these tools.

Assessing the Problem

Often, the request for system implementation might be driven by the emergence of new technologies. It might be based on a regulatory mandate (e.g., infection monitoring or EMRs). On the other hand, it may be to solve an identified problem. A hospital might determine that it needs an operating room scheduling application because of high physician dissatisfaction and time delays in scheduling operating rooms. It is common to blame technology, or the lack of it, for the problem. However, it is spurious to assume, without analysis, that the problem will be solved with the implementation of a surgery scheduling application.

There might, in fact, be other inefficiencies. Until the process and root cause of the problem are appropriately identified and analyzed, it is premature to move toward a technical solution. For example, in the case of a request for a surgery scheduling application to better utilize the operating room and manage patient flow, the issue causing the delays may be that the appropriate supplies are not on the surgical trays or carts when the doctor needs them. This could be the result of poor inventory management, or it might be that the physician's preferences have not been identified, or as is often the case, it may just be poor workflow design or a complete absence of any documented standard workflow. These reasons cannot be uncovered until an objective third party evaluates the process and does some root cause analysis. A common approach to root cause analysis is to use a fishbone (Ishikawa) diagram or to back into the core problem by asking why repeatedly. In the Lean world, this is often called the "five whys." *Five whys* is a technique of asking the question why multiple times to understand the root cause of an issue.

The problem is often not the first and most obvious identified process shortcoming. When an analyst drills down by asking why repeatedly, he or she should ultimately arrive at the root cause of the problem. Often, the root cause will be that there is no understood or documented process or procedure for something. Sadly, it is uncommon for a process assessment to stop a system implementation from going forward. In most organizations, once a project has been selected, and there is momentum, it is rare for the plug to be pulled because a process analyst has determined that the intended system will not fix the problem. However, if the organization's project management structure contains procedures for risk management and issues management (which it should), it is quite reasonable for the analyst to identify this as a risk that project objectives will not be met. It is more likely that the problems identified during the analytical process will merely identify opportunities for the system implementation team to build a system that will truly transform the existing processes, rather than merely automate them.

Documenting the Process

Evaluation and documentation of existing processes can be achieved through individual interviews, group process modeling sessions, or process observation. The output of this exercise is, ideally, a process flow. Figure 6.2 is a process flow of a managed care member appeals process. This process will be described below.

The managed care member appeals process is the process by which a member of a managed care organization who has been denied care for any number of reasons may choose to challenge the managed care organization's decision. As part of a call center implementation at a managed care organization, this process was evaluated to identify the touch points and handoffs between the member, customer service representative (CSR), claims department, and clinical review team. It was one of several processes evaluated as part of a call center implementation project. The objective of the system implementation was to service several different regions of the managed care organization with one centralized call center.

Prior to defining system requirements, it is critical to document existing processes and to identify process improvement opportunities that may or may not be enabled by the new technology. The primary reason for this is to ensure that the system will not be merely automating the existing process. The visual representation of the process is also useful for identifying risks and improvement opportunities and brainstorming future improvements. It can also be used as a schematic to show where systems interact with the process. This can be especially helpful when there are multiple systems that require interface development. Documenting the process supports identification of process improvements before system requirements are developed. Another valid reason for documenting the process with various stakeholders is to engage the future users of the system up front in the design of their workflow, as well as the system. As the future system users work through

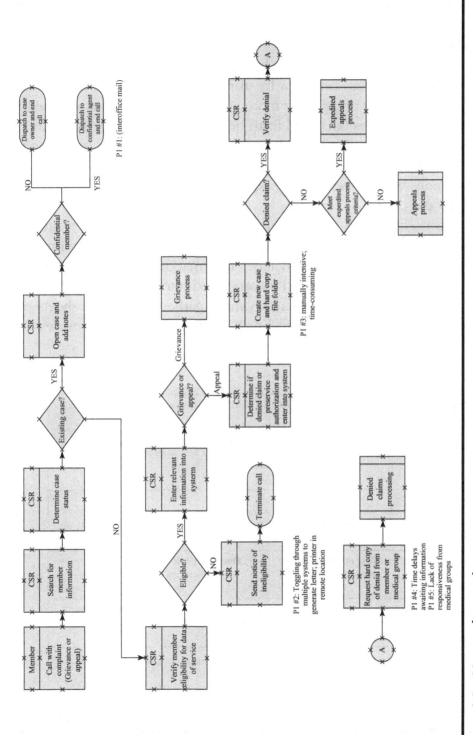

Figure 6.2 Managed care triage process.

their existing process, they will not only identify improvement opportunities, but also begin to envision how the process might be enhanced, so that their contribution to the system requirements development process will be invaluable.

The process flow should show who performs what activity. This can be done by labeling process boxes or by using a cross-functional process flow. Cross-functional flows are slightly more complex to create, but are useful when a process crosses back and forth between multiple functional areas. Cross-functional flows also help identify lag times, or present opportunities for processing that can be parallel, so that one functional area can continue to work fluidly, without necessarily being bound to wait for a handoff from another process.

It is also useful, when documenting processes for the sake of system implementation, to create a matrix that identifies process triggers, inputs, outputs, and metrics. Figure 6.3 includes information that should be captured as part of process assessment and incorporated into the system requirements definition process. Information can be gathered in single sheets per process or, more ideally, in an Excel or Word template or in a business

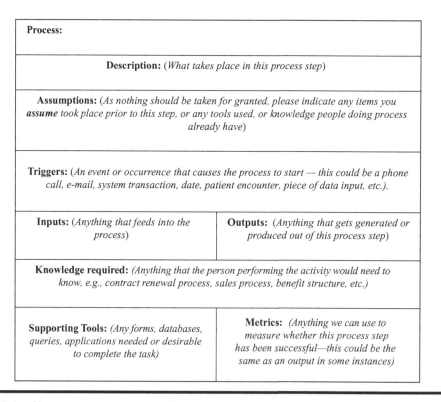

Figure 6.3   Key process components.

process modeling tool. There are a wealth of business process modeling tools available for this purpose, but one should be aware that some of these tools require significant staff training, and unless the tool has an easy-to-use process simulation module, it may not be worth the time and money to get the process team up to speed on using the tool.

Collecting process details may seem like a cumbersome activity, but it is important in the case of a system implementation to understand what triggers a process, all the things that feed into the process (inputs), and the end point (outputs). It is obvious that assumptions should always be captured. A faulty assumption can change everything about a process or about a system design, so it is important to note any assumptions made. The knowledge required by staff or system users and the supporting tools are also important. These latter items feed into the training that will be developed.

Finally, metrics are critical as, presumably, the purpose of the system implementation is to improve a process or the outcome of the process. Since the business case for a system implementation will no doubt include expected benefits, the starting point for those benefits (baseline) must be captured to understand whether the implementation has been a success. It is often difficult to identify or compute a baseline, because a process might be very manual. It could require chart review or process observation to gain an understanding of current state baseline metrics. If a process is being observed, or charts are being reviewed, the reviewer should ensure that a random sample is observed or reviewed and that judgment is not being made based on anomalies.

Identifying and Engaging Stakeholders

Any system implementation in healthcare will have multiple stakeholders, ranging from the end customer, such as the patient, to the physicians, clinicians, unit secretaries, senior management, system users, and others. Often, it may not be clear who all the stakeholders are until the process analysis begins. Typically, this is a top-down process, beginning with the project sponsor and ending with the end user of the process. The frontline workers who are closest to the process may be the best people to help identify other impacted parties. In the process modeled earlier, the key stakeholder is the member who is appealing a health plan decision—either a denial of payment of a claim or a denial of future care (failure to preauthorize care). Other process stakeholders are the member services representatives and physicians and clinicians involved in analyzing the appeal. Typically, the member services organization, claims organization, utilization review, and clinical review may all reside in different areas of the organization.

I was involved in an implementation of this kind where the entire process had been identified and documented, and system requirements definition and rapid application design were scheduled, but the clinical review organization had never been included in the current state documentation or future state visioning. Clearly, it was a key stakeholder, as a patient's file would be forwarded to it for review, and its disposition of the case would need to be routed back to the member services organization to close out the case and inform the member of the results. It is the responsibility of a process analyst or project manager to alert key project sponsors when this kind of oversight is discovered, and to engage the overlooked stakeholders in the remainder of the project. This is not always easy to schedule, and there may be animosity on the part of the party that was excluded. It is therefore critical to interview as many individuals as possible at the outset of a project, and to ensure that all appropriate stakeholders are invited to be involved.

Conducting Interviews

The best way to fully understand the process and stakeholders is to conduct interviews, which is a qualitative form of data collection. It is always best to start with the primary process owner—the individual with the most complete high-level understanding of the flow of a process. Often a process is cross-functional, with several process owners, so it is best to begin with the process owner who has been most closely aligned with the system implementation project, that is, the project sponsor or the project requestor. During the interview process, ask key questions, such as

▪ Who else is involved with this process?
▪ Is there anyone else you think I should be talking to about this process?

Process Modeling Joint Sessions

A process can certainly be documented in pieces, as different process users are interviewed, but if it is clear who the process involves, it is expedient to bring all the stakeholders into a room and facilitate documentation of the process. This can be done manually, getting all the users engaged in documenting their process using Post-it notes on flowchart paper. It can also be done with a projected process flow and one key documenter, who is able to move the process boxes around, as process steps are added and moved. It is always productive to get people energized as they move around the room, but it can be very expedient to document the process live, which eliminates the time required to input the process information after the fact. No matter how the process gets documented, the process flow should include process steps that pose risks or clear process improvement opportunities. The group process modeling sessions can be used instead of or in combination with individual interviews.

Communication Planning

Once it is very clear who is impacted by the process, and how the process might change (improvement opportunities), it is important to begin detailed communication planning as described in Chapter 5 "Project Management". A good communication plan will include a stakeholder assessment. This will look at key stakeholders, the interests of those stakeholders, and the best methods for reaching and communicating with those stakeholders. Once that is understand, the plan should focus on (1) the message to be conveyed; (2) the audience for each message; (3) the timing of the message, that is, when the message should be communicated or at what intervals; (4) the media, or communication vehicle; and (5) the person responsible for delivering the communications. While this may seem obvious and elementary, many projects I have witnessed over the past dozen years neither create nor manage a communication plan. Communication planning is a very iterative process. Communication plans need to be continuously updated throughout the life of the project. A common approach to project communications is to distribute status reports to all impacted stakeholders at regular intervals. This certainly provides necessary information to key stakeholders, but it may not be inclusive of end users; the dilemma is that the status report may be too much detail for an executive and not enough for the end user.

Solidifying the Process Improvement Approach

Once the current state process has been documented and analyzed for improvement opportunities, the organization should solidify its approach to process improvement. A process might give rise to a full-blown "process redesign," which would significantly change the current process, or alternatively, a more focused improvement targeted at the *low-hanging fruit*—those process steps that are the least costly and complex to rapidly improve. Once it is determined which of those two approaches to take, the organization should determine or clarify the desired methodology to use—Lean Six Sigma, old-fashioned process improvement, or some other approach. For a focused improvement, the Lean approach to conducting a three- to five-day rapid improvement event, or Kaizen, could be useful. With a Kaizen event, the proposed changes are put into place as soon as the following week. For larger-scale process improvement, old-fashioned process improvement is useful.

Creating the Future State

There are several steps involved in creating the future state. These include the actual visioning of the future state, as well as the gap analysis between current and future states, validation of system functionality, communications, and marketing of the future state.

Visioning the Solution

Designing a future state process is similar to documenting the current state. Stakeholders should meet in a room with an objective facilitator, who will encourage creative thinking. It is always good to have people put their ideal process on Post-it notes on a flowchart. It is also fun to put people into teams and have each team present its ideal process to the other teams. The objective of the team exercise should be to increase the efficiency of the process, or create a process that enables better data capture or improved patient care. After a team exercise, the group can jointly bring in the best ideas from all of the teams, to create a common best practice process. If the current process clearly documented risks and improvement opportunities, these serve as a springboard for the design of the future process.

The facilitator might target (1) mitigating existing risk, followed by (2) improvement opportunities, as the starting point for the process redesign. It is useful to have a software subject matter expert in the room, who understands the capabilities of the system to be implemented, and who can lend clarity to questions about what the application can do to enable the future state process. For example, if the process involves a step during which the user prints a document and gets up from his or her chair to get an interoffice envelope to route the document, the team might decide that an autosend or alert feature will simplify the process. It is useful to know whether the system is going to autosend the document or an alert, or whether another solution is required. The goal of future state design is always a more efficient and productive process. Figure 6.4 provides an example of the future state for the managed care appeals process.

There are several process improvements identified in the future state workflow in this figure. These are all improvements realized by automating the process or including new system functionality. For example, in the current state workflow, the member calls into the member services call center, and the CSR obtains member information and enters it into the system in order to pull up that member's record. In the new call center system, the member will have entered his or her medical record number (MRN) upon dialing in to the member services center (verbally or by entering numbers on the phone touch pad). That member's information will autopopulate the CSR's computer screen, saving lookup time and avoiding the risk of pulling up information on the wrong member, if there are two members with the same name. In another process step, instead of creating a new hard copy file, the file is created in the system and autorouted to the next agent for processing.

The case will then arrive in the case agent's queue, and the case agent receives an alert that the case is there for processing. This saves processing time for the agent, as well as paper. It also saves the wait time previously incurred while the case was being routed interoffice. Figure 6.4 is an example of a system-driven process improvement and not a radical process improvement or redesign. In this example, the core process was not changed significantly, but improvements would be achieved through automation. There are processes, however, that will lend themselves to a more radical process redesign. The analysis phase of the project will hopefully uncover if a process needs to be redesigned. Good clues that a process itself needs to change considerably include patient, physician, or employee dissatisfaction; redundancy; considerable errors; or long wait times between process steps.

Secure Buy-In

Once a new process has been identified and documented, that process needs to be "shopped" and "marketed" to key stakeholders and process users for validation and input. The people most impacted by the process

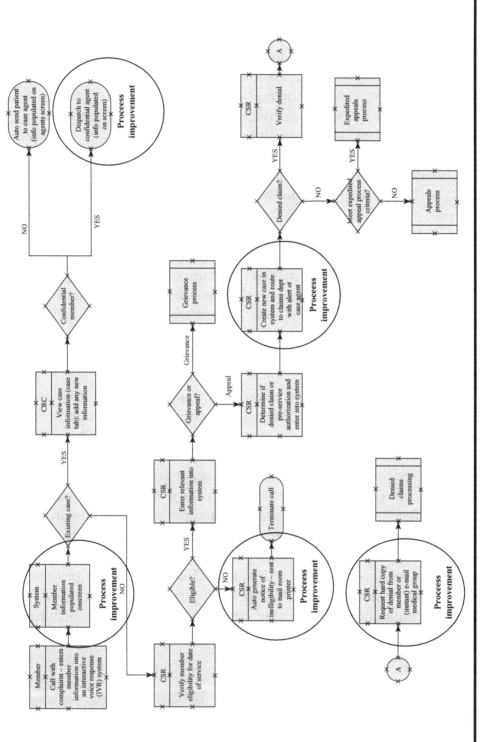

Figure 6.4 Future state of managed care appeals process. IVR.

need to understand the change and support it, understanding how it will impact their workflow. There will always be trepidation, and that's where a gap analysis comes in. The gap analysis, discussed below, will indicate how to address that trepidation. The communication plan will also be instrumental in identifying the message and media to be employed in communicating the message of change.

Identify Metrics and Information Capture Points

Once the future state has been designed, and buy-in secured, a few more steps must be completed before the project team can begin the process of identifying detailed system requirements. The desired metrics must be aligned with the process steps. For example, in the process identified here, you would want to capture the time required to process a member's appeal, especially since the Department of Managed Health Care specifies a required turnaround time. To capture that information, you would want to look at the date of the member's first contact with the health plan and the date the case is closed. It is likely you would also want to measure the disposition of the case, which is likely one data field. In other words, you may want to understand how often appeals are denied or overturned. If appeals are frequently overturned, this might indicate that the initial claims adjudication process is flawed. Interestingly, data captured in one process may provide insights into another related process and point to additional improvement opportunities. In this process example, it might also be useful to tie the case disposition to disease codes, physicians, clinical reviewers, or any number of other data points. This should all be determined as part of the future state design.

If metrics are not considered up front, it could take significant time postimplementation to determine how to capture the required data.

Gap Analysis Definition

Gap analysis is documentation of the gaps between the current state of a process and the desired future state. It focuses on gaps in people, process, and technology. A people gap looks at how people's skills need to change, how people need to be trained, or how people might react to the change. A process change identifies how the process and its related activities or steps differ. A technology change indicates what the new technology will need to do to support the process, or how the new technology differs from the current technology. Figure 6.5 shows a sample gap analysis template for the process identified in the earlier figures.

System Requirements Definition

The technology gaps identified during the gap analysis will feed right into system requirements, while the people and process gaps will feed into the design of training materials and the necessary communications required to secure buy-in. Every organization seems to have a different template or methodology for gathering system requirements. I propose that whichever approach best allows the system developers to build the application to specifications is the best one to use. In the past, when I have worked interactively with developers, I have found it useful to provide a template that ties requirements to each process step. That way, if the development team is unable to fulfill a requirement, it is very easy to go back to the process step impacted and work with the process team to identify a modified process, or to propose a modification to the development team. System requirements are very important for process improvement, to ensure that the steps of process change precede the system requirements definition process. It is certainly possible to develop system requirements without any focus on process, and I would conjecture that it often occurs that way. However, that is what results in a system design that doesn't support or transform the process impacted.

If a project team assesses the current state, designs the future state, and identifies the gaps between the two, the system requirements it identifies

Current State	Future State	People (gap)	Process (gap)	Technology (gap)
Call with complaints (grievance or appeal)	Call with complaints – enters member information into an IVR system	Member required to know MRN or SSN	Shifts identification of member from CSR to member	Need working IVR and automated call recognition
Search for member information	Member information population onscreen	CSR no longer has to search	Process eliminated	Required technology necessary
Determine case status	No process step	CSR needs to update case status. Training necessary	Policies and procedures to be established	A case status fields needs to be included in system.

Figure 6.5 Gap analysis template.

will support the future process and address the gaps between the future and current processes. Too often, a process team throws the requirements "over the wall" to the developer and the system is designed without further input from the process team. I strongly recommend here that the system design be an iterative and interactive process between the developers and process team or process owners.

A *prototype* is a rapid development of a working model that resembles the future state. Prototypes are sometimes developed by a rapid application design approach in which the users and developers are in the room together, if possible. The advantage to keeping the process team engaged throughout system development is that often it is discovered that the system cannot do everything it was assumed up front that it could do. At that point, it might be necessary to modify the process given the constraints of the system. It is only in very rare circumstances that the future state process, as originally conceived, will remain 100% intact.

Summary

System implementation could automate an existing process or transform the process. If there is no attention paid to process improvement in the early phase of the implementation project, the system will merely automate the existing process. Sadly, many existing processes are flawed. By automating an existing process, the ability to improve that process in the future will be hampered by the new system design. Inevitably, thousands, hundreds of thousands, or even millions of dollars were spent on the system implementation, and there will be little, if any, management support for making any changes that will impact the new system. Often, when a system is implemented without a focus on process, significant costs are incurred after the fact, bringing in high-paid consultants to analyze "what went wrong" and to redefine processes that will justify the expense made during the implementation.

The phrase "pay now or pay later" applies to system implementation. By focusing on process, an organization will pay now for the resources required to ensure the process is optimal and supported by the new system. By not including process improvement as part of the implementation, the organization will pay later, not only for consultants, but also for system developers and sometimes even a new system or a new project team. In the latter case, the organization may be paying double or even triple the initial cost of the implementation, especially if the first implementation is abandoned. Process improvement in system implementation is not complex. It is a straightforward process involving process documentation, analysis, future visioning, gap analysis, and communication and change management planning. It requires that the process team and system developers work together. Ensuring that process improvement is part of an implementation supports user adoption and eliminates project overages and post-project expense fixing everything that was not addressed during implementation. Process improvement is a little bit of work that eliminates a lot of future pain.

Key Terms

Current state, five whys, future state, gap, gap analysis, low-hanging fruit, process, process redesign, prototype

Discussion Questions

1. What are the primary goals of process redesign?
2. What are the best ways to judge the improvements made in a future state?
3. How can a prototype help improve process improvement?

References

Alter A (2007). CIOs rank their top priorities for 2008. *CIO Insight*, December 20.
Chang J (2017). *Business Process Management Systems*. Boca Raton, FL: Taylor & Francis group.

DATA ANALYTICS AND POPULATION HEALTH

Healthcare has the potential for significant improvements for organizations and the community. Data, converted into useful information, is one way that better decisions for patients, organizations, and society can be made. Big data has been talked about as a panacea. But what do we do with all these data we are collecting? Skills in data analysis are extremely essential, since the data themselves do not produce change. Sharing of that information, and sometimes between organizations that are not even part of our own four walls, is the only way to create systemic changes. Population health management is also essential to long-term improvements. Quality management and performance improvement professionals will be expected to lead in each of these areas. In this section, we focus on the role of data analytics, collaboration, and population health as drivers of performance improvement.

Chapter 7

Big Data, Predictive Modeling, and Collaboration

James Langabeer

Contents

The true sign of intelligence is not knowledge but imagination.

Dr. Albert Einstein
Physicist

Introduction

The healthcare industry has a way to go before it can claim the efficiency and quality of other service industries, such as retail or hospitalities. We can see this clearly when we look at one simple example—wait times in the typical urban emergency department (Wiler et al., 2017). As an example, there are somewhere around a quarter billion visits to emergency departments across the nation on a yearly basis. Only about 25% of these have acceptable wait times, as reported by the Centers for Disease Control and Prevention in 2016. Similarly, the National Academy of Medicine (formerly the Institute of Medicine) outlined in a groundbreaking report the crisis in healthcare, and how improvements are necessary in both operational and information flows (National Academy of Medicine, 2006).

So why has healthcare been slow to respond to improvements? Obviously, there are multiple reasons, but here I focus on the most prominent ones:

■ Lack of transparent and actionable information (sometimes referred to as big data)
■ Inability to make decisions and predictions based on these data
■ Lack of interorganizational collaboration in the industry

Big Data

The lack of accessible information is obviously important. While the Department of Health and Human Services' Office of the National Coordinator for Health Information Technology (ONC) has invested billions of dollars into providers' adoption of electronic health records (EHRs), there has still been little sharing of that information beyond the walls of a single provider.

In hospitals and health systems, a significant majority of large urban facilities have implemented an EHR. Epic, Cerner, Meditech, Allscripts, Athena, and many other technology companies provide enterprise-level systems across the country. Many of the 6,000+ hospitals and nearly 250,000 physician practices in the United States alone also have systems in place.

Yet, with these systems, the data contained are largely restricted to a singular practice or site and are not available to the public, consumers, or industry analysts. Compare that with consumer goods industries, where everything that is known about a product is made available to others. Prices and costs are established. Components and ingredients are disclosed. The availability of specific brands is in plain sight. Manufacturers, distributors, and retailers regularly share inventory, pricing, and promotion information through *electronic data interchange* (EDI). EDI is a process that allows organizations to share key pieces of data through standardized electronic means.

With all this movement toward digital health records, there is ample information available for predictive and prescriptive decision making, that is, using these data to drive improved operations and better decisions (Langabeer and Helton, 2016). Since organizations are evolving toward methods such as Six Sigma (which requires data modeling), there will be potential for significantly greater use of big data in the future.

Process improvement is fundamentally about understanding underlying data. This means identifying behavior, trends, and patterns over time. Data offer administrators and providers with a clearer understanding of what is really occurring in their organizations. Analytical models can transform these data into actionable strategies and decisions to drive improvements.

Big data refers to extremely large data sets that can be analyzed to reveal trends and patterns. Big data is formally defined as having three key characteristics: volume, variety, and velocity (McAfee and Brynjolfsson, 2012; Ghosh, 2016). In healthcare, volume would indicate the number of patients, genes, samples, or data points in a data set. Variety would refer to the types of data available, including insurance claims, patient health records, radiological images, or other types of data. The velocity of health data represents the timing and intensity of the data generated, and how quickly it changes.

Big data has been applied in retail for dozens of years. Large retailers such as Best Buy or Walmart have routinely collected granular levels of detail. Notice the register receipt the next time you visit a retailer. You will see codes that define the transaction identification, cashier, specific items sold, prices, use of discounts or promotions, coupon codes, and many other pieces of data. Retail systems can translate these data into useful information, which can help determine when to add staff or use promotions.

Data analytics has significant potential to help improve daily decision making and organizational and patient outcomes (Bates et al., 2014). The widespread adoption and usage of EHRs makes data availability less of a concern. However, there are many other issues besides availability.

- Can you overcome security and privacy issues for the organization?
- Can you get access to the data, physically?
- Can you extract or export the data into a usable format for modeling or analysis?
- Can you get your organization's information systems personnel to help you pull and format the data?
- Do you have the knowledge and expertise to handle the data, once extracted? Although trivial, there could be millions of rows of data in a data set. Even having access to a software tool that can manage all these data, let alone transform them and integrate them into a modeling software, is a real concern for most people that are not informaticians by training.

These are significant challenges remaining with big data, but they can be overcome. Quality and performance improvement experts are key to making this happen. One of the ways to best utilize big data is to help improve decisions through decision modeling.

Decision Models

Decision models help to forecast the future so that better decisions can be made. A *decision* is a choice between two or more alternatives. Predictive models support management and clinical decision making, and follow a decision analysis approach. *Decision analysis* is the process of separating or decomposing a complex decision, and incorporating uncertainty and dynamic assumptions into algorithms to generate alternative choices. Alternatively, it can also be described as the use of analytic methods to make better decisions. The process of decision modeling involves framing the decision to be made, and then structuring a quantitative approach to evaluate choices. This decision model has several key steps, shown in Figure 7.1.

Decision models take many forms. One of those is predictive modeling.

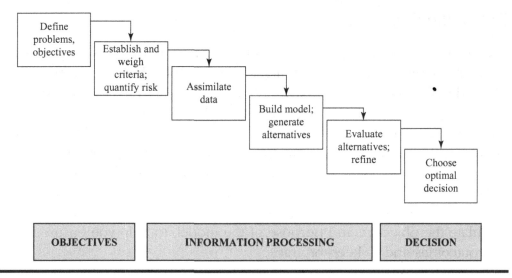

Figure 7.1 Decision analysis.

Predictive Modeling

The *New York Times* ran a story that described Walmart's use of other types of data as well (such as weather) to better predict demand and increase revenue. Using the possibility of a hurricane, the retailer determined that specific items were linked to increases in sales (Hays, 2004). With this estimate or forecast, the retailer could order more inventory to avoid the inventory being out of stock when a customer arrives. *Predictive modeling* is the use of an algorithm and software on large data sets to forecast potential outcomes. Predictive modeling is one form of decision modeling. An *algorithm* is a formula or calculation used to solve a problem in the model.

In healthcare, there is a tremendous opportunity to use big data for predictive modeling. For example, we could use patient acute care data to better determine staffing levels on an hourly basis for a facility. We could better understand which insurance companies were more effective from a revenue cycle perspective. We could use estimates of lengths of stay to help schedule potential room turnovers. Most importantly, we could use data to identify how to improve patient safety and eliminate medical errors.

Predictive modeling is completely aligned with the plan–do–check–act (PDCA) improvement methodology described earlier. It involves planning for a potential future outcome. There are multiple steps involved in predictive modeling, starting by defining the objective.

Define the Objective

The first step to predicting optimal solutions is to understand what you are trying to optimize. Although that might sound simple, there are many cases where decision modelers and decision makers get mired in details of big data and end up solving a different problem than they had intended. Carefully examine what you are trying to predict: Is your organization trying to predict future length of stay? Identify potential days with the highest rate of infections? Look for the best possible mix of payers to improve financial performance?

Is the problem one of maximization (e.g., patient throughput), minimization (wait times), or optimization (best use of constrained resources)? Clearly articulate the objective and purpose of the model, to help you ensure the best outcomes and to keep on track.

Data Collection and Cleansing

Start by identifying the primary data sources available and necessary to help solve the problem. Are those data in your time and labor system? In the EHR? Enterprise resource planning (ERP) system? Ensure which data points you are looking for, and which variables specifically.

Collect the data, whether through integration from another system or an extract (export) from that system. Ensure that the data are cleaned. *Data cleansing* is a process of validating and fixing incomplete, inaccurately coded, or corrupt data. Transformation involves making changes to data where appropriate to ensure that all the data can be used. This includes arranging the data in a usable manner and coding all variables consistently for analysis.

Preliminary Review

Once the data are in one place, start by using some form of graphical analysis to display the data. This could be through creating run charts, Pareto analysis, tabular displays, geospatial maps, or anything similar you are comfortable with. Examine the data for trends and patterns, or process behavior that is statistically out of process control. If you are examining payer reimbursements by diagnosis-related group (DRG), plot the data and examine if they appear valid. Ensure that you have somebody on the team that knows the data well, to ensure they have been extracted, transformed, and presented properly. Remember that data variability should be noted. This initial graphical analysis ensures that the data you are basing your predictions on appear consistent and reliable.

Apply Algorithms

Depending on the software you choose, either utilize the existing algorithm or use your own algorithm. There are many different types, but three of the most widely used are summative, linear programming, and regressions. This book is not the place to find details of the math behind any algorithms, because generally organizations choose a software program that has embedded the algorithm already. For instance, if you use a tool (such as Monte Carlo simulation software), the solution will have its own calculation engine that uses probability distributions and sampling techniques. However, if you choose to utilize a spreadsheet or other database, you might need to build a formula. Sometimes, a straightforward solution to predictive modeling is to use a regression technique, which examines the relationship between certain independent variables and the outcome you are seeking to model. This can be done in Excel, or in analytical software (such as SAS or SPSS), as well as many others.

For example, maybe you are looking to see if you can understand what drives long patient wait times in your emergency department. You have collected extensive data, and believe that wait times are a reflection of inadequate staffing or resources. If you use a simple formula where you look for changes in what is driving patient wait times, you could apply a formula such as this one:

$$Y = B_0 + B_1 \times X_1 + B_2 \times X_2 + e$$

where:
Y = wait times
B_0 = nurse staffing ratios
B_1 = available beds
e = error

In this formula, X are the observations (the data points) for each of the attributes (or variables) represented by beta (B) values. Using the data, you could produce a prediction of Y (wait times) using all the assumptions and data. These types of algorithm fit (or determine) a mathematical solution where the beta multiplied by the parameter estimate (and then added with the other variables) sums to an optimal value for the outcome (Y).

Using a statistical tool for regression, models can use a combination of stepwise adjustment to add or remove variables that do not add to the overall predictive capacity or goodness of fit. Getting the right mix of important variables, and then fitting those variables with the correct coefficients, is the science and art of modeling. This requires focus and significant fine-tuning.

Validate Results

Examine and validate the initial results. Do they correspond generally with the expected results? Are they in line with what you thought you would see? If you thought the outcome would be in a valid range (let's say 1–10) and your prediction comes out as a negative value, that would indicate that you need to go back and validate and refine the model.

Validation is used in modeling to describe the act of ensuring that the model reflects reality. Validation should always occur by sharing results with the decision makers and people most knowledgeable about the practice and the data. If you are modeling a surgery department, make sure you have the surgical management team and chief surgeon involved in validation. All models need fine-tuning and validation.

Apply Prediction to Decisions

Once you have an estimate or prediction of future outcomes, you need to incorporate them into your decision-making process. If you have predictions of when staffing needs to be increased, to keep up with patient volumes, it is necessary to share that information and to make sure future labor schedules and rosters are in place.

Figure 7.2 summarizes the steps involved in predictive modeling.

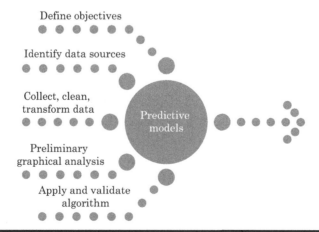

Figure 7.2 Steps in predictive modeling.

CASE STUDY

Barbara Smith, an analyst at Watertown Hospital, is attempting to predict the impact of a change on the financial performance of the organization. The CEO has asked for the data from the balanced scorecard to be used to determine which factors are most responsible for driving changes in operating margins (income from operations divided by total revenue). Many data points were collected, including the strategic, operating, environmental, and internal processes.

The organization decided to use a statistical package to model the data. Data were imported. A regression technique was used to fit the variables into a prediction model for the operating margin. Barbara noticed that most of the variables had values that were not in the statistically significant range, so they were stepwise removed from the model. The model ended with four variables that were significant for the organization. The model is

$$Y = B_0 + B_1 \times X_1 + B_2 \times X_2 + B_3 \times X_3 + B_4 \times X_4 + e$$

Variable	Attribute	Weight (B)	Value	Estimate
B1	Adjusted patient days	0.034	100	3.4
B2	Market share	0.382	6	2.292
B3	Average length of stay	0.08	6.0	0.48
B4	Labor productivity	0.025	5	0.125
Y	Operating margin			**6.297**

Based on the weighted values of the four attributes, the predictive model generated a 6.3% operating margin and provided an estimate of the other four variables. The analyst compared this with the past and determined that the error of the model was low.

Once the model was established, the estimates for each of the four variables could be simply modeled. With this new tool, management could perform "what if" scenarios to estimate changes in key variables that might influence their overall results.

As Barbara discovered, for example, if the average adjusted patient days increases by just 5% (from 100,000 per year in the table above), the operating margin could change to 6.46%. Changes in length of stay, labor productivity, and market share could all be simulated to predict potential change in operating margin. Of course, Barbara cautioned management that any shift in a certain variable (like patient days) might also increase other variables (such as market share), so there is not always a strict ability to isolate changes in only one variable. That is why predictive modeling is only a tool.

Barbara's model was well received by the CEO and management team at Watertown Hospital, since it gave them a tool to begin strategic discussions around decisions and priorities.

Information Sharing beyond Organizational Walls

It is one thing to collect and analyze data that are stored and maintained in your own organization. Security and governance processes typically allow for employees to gain de-identified access to appropriate data to help make quality improvements. But as we learned in Chapter 1, quality management is about "systemic" change. Often, that means that we need to include either vendors or other partners in process improvement projects. That is where we get true complexity!

Collaboration between organizations has been widely discussed between for-profit organizations that seek to work together toward common goals. A typical health partnership could involve the emergency medical services (EMS) defining better joint processes with local hospital emergency departments. It could also entail organizations' materials management departments working with vendors to better understand material usage and inventory requirements. There are many times that healthcare clinics or hospitals will need to reach out to other organizations to truly solve a problem and improve performance.

Collaboration between different organizations is sometimes referred to as strategic alliance. A *strategic alliance* is a loosely coupled arrangement between distinct organizations to fulfill a larger, usually more long-term purpose. These are also called partnerships. Most strategic alliances are used between two hospitals that are not owned by the same health system, but are working collaboratively together for a joint purpose, such as to expand to a new geographic region.

Collaboration is the process of working with another entity. Collaboration in a single organization is often referred to as teamwork. Teamwork applied across organizations is usually called a partnership. However, teamwork between departments motivated by the same executives and vision is sometimes simpler than working across organizational boundaries. Different organizations have different management styles, cultures, performance goals, and expectations. These differences are problematic when you are trying to improve a process across organizations.

Interorganizational Collaboration

Interorganizational collaborations are partnerships sought to improve the competitive advantage for the respective parties or organizations involved. Yet in healthcare, most of the research shared involves findings from a single organization. Little is known about how to work together through partnerships. This is a significant opportunity for improvement.

In one of our projects we worked to bring together a large group of hospitals and EMS agencies to create a regionalized integrated system of care (Langabeer et al., 2017). A system of care is a collaborative network of entities that work together across a region in a coordinated fashion to improve processes and outcomes across a continuum of care. Systems of care usually refer to organizations that are not part of the same integrated delivery system, although this is not a requirement. Improving the coordination between certain organizations (such as a referral hospital and a cardiac receiving center) is essential to improving the overall treatment times in a community.

Theories behind the motivation and barriers to interorganizational collaboration help to describe why certain organizations (those that are sometimes competing for patients and financial resources) choose to collaborate in the first place. In metropolitan regions, hospitals and other healthcare facilities deploy competitive strategies to increase patient volumes, quality, and margins. Hospital competition, even for nonprofit organizations, is so intense that managerial tactics emphasize identifying and targeting certain payer groups and service lines. This rivalry is often seen as contradictory to collaboration.

If you are involved in a community project beyond your own organizational walls, what should you do differently? Well, first understand the motivations behind the individuals in the room. There will be many different reasons. Some organizations are seeking to improve their credibility. Some are seeking financial gain. Some are trying to differentiate their services. Some might be trying to learn from you!

There are several issues that emerge in the political and organizational realm—fear of sharing confidential information, for example. Fear of speaking in front of new individuals. Concern around how feedback will get to your manager. There are several key ingredients for working across organizations that everyone should know about, including trust, transparency, transfer, and teamwork.

Trust is essential to the process. Trusting others in the room and the legitimacy of the project itself leads to genuine conversation and disclosure. Teamwork is also necessary. Working together, and not alone or in silos, produces better results. Groups of individuals working together will produce better ideas and solutions for large-scale problems than an individual. Transparency is also key. *Transparency* is an attribute of being clear, so that things can be seen distinctly. Transparency involves sharing of information about business and clinical practices. Transfer is the ability to provide information openly between parties. Simply put, this means being able to talk. Talking in front of new groups and people is sometimes difficult for analysts, but this is essential to producing the kind of process changes necessary on a community level or between organizations. Figure 7.3 summarizes these building blocks.

If you can master these building blocks, and then apply the same analytical process rigor as you would in any other project, you can achieve great results.

Health Information Exchange

Sharing information beyond organizational boundaries requires a different type of collaboration and data set. Community-based projects often involve multiple organizations coming together to address a larger issue—such as a stroke system or a homeless program. There needs to be a way to get access to information across these organizational lines.

Figure 7.3 Building blocks for interorganizational projects.

One of the most interesting mechanisms for sharing data is the *health information exchange* (HIE). HIE is a technology infrastructure that enables secure digital exchange of standardized information across organizations involved in the care of a patient (HIMSS, 2017).

Unlike consumer goods industries (which routinely share information between manufacturers and stores), healthcare has been a laggard in digital technologies with regards to interoperability. Providers often need access to a patient's medical records from prior visits elsewhere. Payers could benefit from knowing about transactional details prior to their coverage. Administrators could utilize patient information in self-population forms to avoid redundancy in all business processes. Yet despite the potential, there has not been significant progress toward interorganizational technology in health.

Community-based, regional HIE organizations evolved in response to federal aims to encourage interoperability, yet little is known about their strategic approach (Langabeer and Champagne-Langabeer, 2013). An HIE is dedicated to managing and transferring a patient's health and administrative data (such as records, images, and results). Storage of these data points is necessary to share (collaborate) between different providers to improve the delivery of care. Some health systems have created their own private extension of the EHR, which is one form of HIE. Integrated delivery systems need a tool to manage across their different sites and locations. The second way is the community-based, regional organizations.

Rising costs, increased medical errors, and lack of coordination in care for patients between facilities have risen to dangerous levels in the U.S. healthcare economy. There have been multiple health policy initiatives designed to improve the overall health system delivery performance, but very few have garnered as much momentum as policies surrounding health information technology. Technology and system interoperability are often seen as solutions for the healthcare system.

The EHR has existed since the 1950s, and over time hospitals and physician practices have been slowly adopting these systems. Getting all providers on digital platforms is first necessary if we are to successfully transfer information between organizations. Yet, the adoption of these in all practices and systems has lagged for many reasons, including the following:

- *Cost*: Most systems cost significant sums of money for initial capital, as well as ongoing maintenance.
- *Physician dissatisfaction*: Many providers have historically favored written text or transcribed notes over entry into a computerized system.

Workflow often takes longer for a physician than simply dictating to a nurse or a device.

■ *Incentive*: There is not a great incentive to transition to an EHR. While the data are stored electronically versus on paper, the actual financial incentives to transition are not there.

■ *Privacy*: There is always a concern about inappropriate access, or breach, of a patient's medical records. Security and privacy are top-level concerns.

Despite these barriers, the EHR is now in place with nearly all the major hospitals in the United States, and well over half of all physician offices. Since this is a requirement before they can be shared in an HIE, it was necessary to invest in these resources to get most providers technologically prepared. Now, as most providers are on an electronic system, it is time to begin using these systems for performance improvement across communities.

The multiple *potential* benefits of electronically sharing patient health information between providers have been well documented. We say "potential" because we are not seeing widespread utilization yet of the HIE. Benefits can include improved care coordination, reduced duplication of tests and scans, and improved efficiencies. Yet there are delivery and organizational barriers that continue to plague the path toward interoperability. Figure 7.4 shows the conceptual HIE framework.

Some of you may remember discussions of community health information networks (CHINs) or regional health information organizations (RHIOs). The modern HIE has evolved from those initial efforts. Now, however, there are structural differences that should drive increases in HIE. These include

■ *Adoption*: As we mentioned, a significant majority of all hospitals and practices have adopted EHR systems to date.

■ *Industry standards*: There has been significant progress in electronic standards to support interoperability, including HL7, IHE, XCA, and LOINC.

■ *Compliance with standards*: EHR vendors are coding and integrating these standards into their systems.

■ *Economics*: There have been incentive payments from the Centers for Medicare and Medicaid Services (CMS) that offer "Meaningful Use" credits and payments. These financial incentives have helped to change the

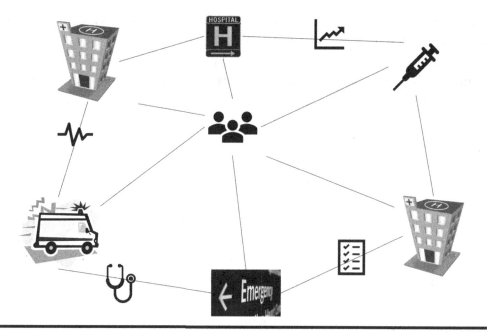

Figure 7.4   Health information exchange.

economics. In addition, there have been changes in health plan payer reimbursement that support the sharing of information.

■ *Mutual collaboration*: There seems to be a more collaborative nature between most parties in the healthcare value chain.

■ *Techno-savvy users*: The users of technology (physicians and nurses) utilize a smartphone daily for their personal affairs. So, the use of technology in a healthcare setting is much more acceptable and routine.

■ *Need*: There are many projects where organizations need access to big data—data that are outside of their own control. Obtaining this information easily is the role of the HIE.

■ *Patient mobility*: Patients are much more likely now to visit multiple providers and facilities. In years past, patient loyalty was higher and they were likely to stick with only one doctor or hospital. Times have changed, and patient mobility is driving a need for HIE.

There are many large regional HIEs operating in the country. A few of the more notable ones include the Regenstrief Institute in Indiana, the Statewide Health Information Network for New York (SHIN-NY), Greater Houston Healthconnect, and the Colorado Regional Health Information Organization. Larger regions probably all have some form of HIE in progress. Data availability varies by region and vendor, but most have a combination of data. There is a range of value and complexity to the different types of data, as shown in Figure 7.5.

HIEs are one way that quality improvement analysts will obtain data in the future. Getting to know your community-based HIE representatives is a good idea, to understand which data types are available.

Summary

Information is necessary to drive performance improvement. In larger and more complex projects, different organizations might be involved. Interorganizational collaboration is necessary to form partnerships with other organizations in the community for a joint strategic purpose. Trust, transparency, transfer, and teamwork are all skills necessary for quality improvement analysts. Big data will help in these types of projects, and support decision making. Predictive modeling is one useful technique of decision analysis that can use these data to forecast possible outcomes. An HIE represents the future of sharing information across multiple organizations.

Key Terms

Big data, data cleansing, decision, decision analysis, electronic data interchange, interorganizational collaboration, health information exchange, predictive modeling, strategic alliances, system of care, teamwork, transparency, validation

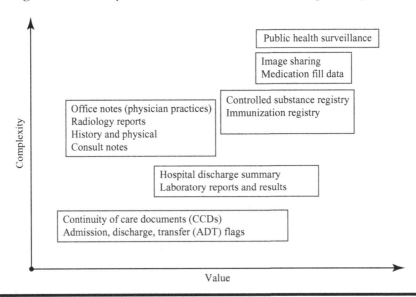

Figure 7.5   Data value and complexity in HIE.

Discussion Questions

1. What is the real difference between data and big data?
2. Describe as many types of decisions that you can envision a healthcare system making that might require a decision model?
3. What steps in predictive modeling involve fine-tuning your assumptions?
4. How can strategic partnerships between organizations be used for quality improvement?
5. What are the barriers to building interorganizational collaboration?

References

Bates DW, Saria S, Ohno-Machado L, Shah L, and Escobar G (2014). Big data in health care: Using analytics to identify and manage high-risk and high-cost patients. *Health Affairs*, 33, 71123–71131.

Centers for Disease Control and Prevention (2016). Emergency department fast facts. Available at http://www.cdc.gov/nchs/fastats/emergency-department.htm.

Ghosh R (2016). Healthcare and big data: Hype or unevenly distributed future? *Analytics*, November/December, 20–23.

Hays C (2004). What Walmart knows about customers' habits. *New York Times*, November 14. http://www.nytimes.com/2004/11/14/business/yourmoney/what-walmart-knows-about-customers-habits.html.

HIMSS (Healthcare Information and Management Systems Society) (2017). *HIMSS Dictionary of Health Information Technology Terms, Acronyms, and Organizations*. 4th edn. Boca Raton, FL: Taylor & Francis/CRC Press.

Langabeer J and Champagne-Langabeer T (2013). The evolution of health information exchange. *Journal of Healthcare Information Management*, 27(2), 24–30.

Langabeer J, Champagne-Langabeer T, Helton J, Segrest W, Kash B, DelliFraine J, and Fowler R (2017). Interorganizational collaboration in emergency cardiovascular care. *Quality Management in Healthcare*, 26(1), 1–6.

Langabeer J and Helton J (2016). *Health Care Operations Management: A Systems Perspective*. Boston: Jones and Bartlett.

McAfee A and Brynjolfsson E (2012). Big data: The management revolution. *Harvard Business Review*, October.

National Academy of Medicine (2006). *The Future of Emergency Care: Key Findings and Recommendations*. Washington, DC: National Academy of Sciences.

Wiler J, Pines J, and Ward MJ, eds. (2017). *Value and Quality Innovations in Acute and Emergency Care*. Cambridge: Cambridge University Press.

Chapter 8

Analytics in Healthcare Organizations

Jeffrey R. Helton

Contents

> Quality has to be caused, not controlled.
>
> **Philip B. Crosby**
> *Quality Guru*

Introduction

Many management challenges in the healthcare industry can be addressed by analyzing readily available clinical and business data. Healthcare providers gather significant amounts of data on a routine basis, but do not make use of those data to analyze and understand organizational performance or to find ways to improve performance. Using simple analytical techniques, managers can identify patterns of resource utilization or associate payments with costs and find significant opportunities to improve profitability or quality of patient care.

Analytical Challenges

Kevin Rogers took his seat in his office as the new chief operating officer for Community Medical Center. As he started to peruse the reports presented to him daily, he noticed a summary of insurer payments and saw that there were some accounts paid for patients served by a newly recruited orthopedic surgeon. He noted that there appeared to be quite a bit of volume coming from this physician and the accounts appeared to be paid in a timely manner. So far, so good. Then he moved along to reviewing some invoices requiring approval for payment. Near the top of that stack, Kevin saw an invoice for implantable prosthetics, many of which were used on surgical cases by that newly recruited orthopedic surgeon. Out of curiosity, Kevin looked at some of the prices the hospital was charged for these items used as a part of surgeries performed by the new orthopedic surgeon. An unusual fact caught his attention—the invoice price for those orthopedic implants was about as much as the payment received for the surgeries he noted only a few moments before. "How could this be?" he asked himself as a great state of concern and confusion built up inside him. He wondered, "Is it possible that we could be losing money on much of the patient volume being generated by this new orthopedic surgeon? What could management be missing here?" Kevin pulled up the day's operating room schedule and noticed that this newly recruited physician appeared prominently throughout the day in one operating room. Suddenly, Kevin started to feel a sense of dread.

It is Monday morning, and Tiffany James comes into her office as chief executive officer of High Country Health Plan. As she settled into the morning routine, she noted in her web news headline feed that a local physician had just been indicted for billing fraud by state Medicaid officials. She paused for a moment because that name sounded somewhat familiar to her. Opening her weekly claims payment report, she found that same physician's name near the top of the list of largest claim payment amounts for the prior week. She suddenly started to wonder how much in those payments might be similarly fraudulent. "How could it be that other insurers have discovered this and her plan had not?" she asked herself. She reached for her keyboard to send an e-mail to the health plan claims director to get more details.

These two scenarios point out common problems that face healthcare managers in today's marketplace. In each case, an ongoing program of data analysis—asking questions about the utilization of resources and the efficiency and effectiveness of operational operations, and seeking ways to improve patient care—is becoming an essential tool in running a successful healthcare business. The challenges facing managers in this industry call for the ability to analyze data and understand what is happening in the business.

The healthcare system in the United States in the early twenty-first century might reasonably be labeled to be in a state of great disarray. Policy makers, healthcare providers, and government policy makers struggle with the conflicting priorities of providing good patient care at a reasonable price within a financing system that is sustainable for the broader economy. Considering that the U.S. healthcare system currently consumes nearly 18% of the nation's economic output (Kaiser Family Foundation, 2017), the prospect of healthcare cannibalizing resources from other essential parts of the economy is a great policy concern. At the same time, reducing payments to providers to stem the rate of growth of healthcare in the economy poses a risk of taking resources away from meeting essential patient care needs. Thus, our current healthcare system faces several vexing dilemmas, primarily how to deliver care that meets generally accepted standards of quality, at a lower cost to the economy?

Fundamental to our healthcare system is the gathering of detailed documentation of services provided to patients for each occasion of service. The healthcare system for decades has gathered enormous volumes of data on patients and then systematically filed them away in archives. This store of useful data has remained essentially unused in understanding the business of healthcare for decades. Since passage of the Health Information Technology for Economic and Clinical Health (HITECH) Act in 2009, the industry has started to move toward gathering that patient care data in a form that can be analyzed, referred to as *structured data* (Hoyt and Yoshihashi, 2014). The advent of electronic health records (EHRs) has converted our old practice of creating data on paper (*unstructured data*) and relying on manual review of paper records to the new norm of documenting patient data using structured data. This gives managers in the industry greater resources to use in understanding what is happening in the organization and to find ways to improve performance.

But why bother to analyze performance in healthcare organizations? The passing of the Patient Protection and Affordable Care Act (ACA) in 2010 set the stage for healthcare providers (e.g., hospitals, physicians, and clinics) to be held to standards of demonstrating patient care quality, while doing so at reduced fees. Private insurers quickly followed suit. Payment reductions were further exacerbated by the implementation of quality penalties for hospital providers if certain levels of patient care process were not documented in the case of Medicare patients (Kaiser Family Foundation, 2013). Commercial insurers have also similarly implemented such quality process penalties. Further, as was illustrated in the opening scenario, tracking utilization of resources is essential in maintaining profitable operations. As described in the first scenario mentioned at the beginning of this chapter, being able to track the cost and volume of patient care resources is an essential management exercise in today's environment of tightly constrained payments.

Using another example presented at the beginning of this chapter, a health plan could easily protect its resources from fraudulent or ineffective services by tracking resource utilization and perhaps profiling the utilization of resources by providers in its network. Being able to review payments for patterns of unusual behavior or to compare utilization among providers can help a health plan protect the integrity of its claims adjudication process and keep medical costs low for its customers.

The Value of Analytics in Healthcare

The focus of this chapter is therefore to introduce the reader to the types of analyses useful in today's healthcare industry, to discuss the sources and types of data available, to give a brief synopsis of the types of analyses that can be useful to healthcare managers, to define performance metrics that can be tracked on an ongoing basis, and finally, to apply these analytic tools to other established performance improvement programs, such as dashboards and Six Sigma, and ensure compliance with federal value-based purchasing requirements.

Healthcare businesses can use the data they routinely gather to make necessary changes to operations that will improve profitability and patient care. This analysis is referred to as *analytics*. Analytics involves the use of available business data to understand operational performance, resource utilization, and costs of patient care, and using such information to support managers in making critical decisions about operations (Strome, 2013). While healthcare has been using computer systems for decades, it has only been in the last 10 years that provider organizations have gathered data specific to patient care in a computerized format that can be easily combined with financial data to gain much greater insight into organizational performance.

Types of Data in Healthcare Organizations

Healthcare organizations have a wealth of data available to them to conduct very productive and insightful analytic work. The centerpiece of this analytics "toolbox" is the *electronic medical record*. The electronic medical record replaces much of the paper record keeping that has been used by healthcare providers for decades. However, the electronic medical record is not the only source of patient care data. Other applications that can be used in healthcare analytics include radiology information systems (RISs), picture archival and communication systems (PACSs), medication administration records (MARs), laboratory information systems (LISs), and pharmacy information systems (RxISs) (Glandon et al., 2013). The combination of the clinical documentation applications described here is the EHR. All these applications gather data specific to the care of the patient: the clinical signs and symptoms evidenced by the patient, plans for treatment, and evaluation of treatment outcomes— referred to as *clinical data* (Wager et al., 2013).

Essential to managing the business affairs of a healthcare organization is an entirely different set of applications aimed at operational functions, such as billing and collection, purchasing and inventory of clinical supplies, payroll, and claims adjudication and accounts payable systems. The patient demographics, cost of supply, and cost of labor data gathered by these applications are commonly referred to as *administrative data* (Wager et al., 2013).

Administrative and clinical data are both essential elements in healthcare analytics projects. The challenge is understanding what data elements reside in which area. Table 8.1 summarizes some common types of administrative and clinical data elements.

The combination of clinical and administrative data is often needed to answer management questions such as, how much does it cost to take care of a hip replacement, or which physician has the best outcomes for invasive cardiology? Usually, the clinical and administrative data needed to answer these types of questions reside in different application databases. Trying to join the data from these disparate applications may be a challenge to completing an analytics project. However, most administrative and clinical applications are joined together through a common database, known as the *master patient index* (MPI). Within the MPI, patient demographics are usually captured in one place and shared with other applications—both clinical and administrative—used within a healthcare organization. The MPI captures patient name, other demographic information, and a unique patient identification number used within the organization. That identification number in the MPI can be used to join data for a specific patient or group of patients across administrative and clinical application databases. Figure 8.1 presents a high-level view of these myriad applications and their data-sharing relationships.

Table 8.1 Examples of Clinical and Administrative Data

Administrative Data	*Clinical Data*
Patient identification	Patient identification
Patient name	Height and weight
Patient data of birth	Onset of current illness
Patient home address	Past illness history
Insurance plan data	Blood pressure
Insurance plan payment terms	Diagnostic test and medication orders
Insurance authorization terms	Diagnostic test values
Labor hours paid for caregivers	Medications administered
Pay rates for staff	Procedures performed
Supply inventory levels	Diagnostic impressions
Invoice cost of patient care supplies	Outcomes of treatment and future care plans

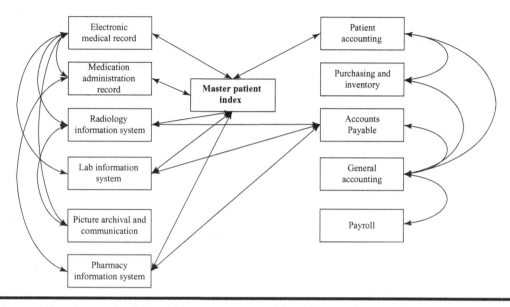

Figure 8.1   General relationships among provider information applications.

From the health plan perspective, there certainly will be less clinical data gathered since the health plan primarily acts as a vehicle for financing payments to healthcare providers on behalf of patients. However, there is limited gathering of clinical data in a health plan for purposes of utilization management and coordination of care among provider groups, usually for patients with chronic conditions, such as high blood pressure or asthma. Administrative applications used by health plan organizations would be like those described earlier, but will focus primarily on claims adjudication systems that will gather significant amounts of data from claims for payment sent by healthcare providers to the insurer. In addition, the MPI used by providers would be replaced with a membership or enrollment database that would serve the same function of describing patient demographic data, but also include the dates between which a health plan would be obligated to pay for services on behalf of the patient. A simple diagram of these applications is shown in Figure 8.2.

The medical claim form normally used in the healthcare industry today includes basic clinical information that can help to guide analytics projects as well. Data from the medical claim form can be obtained from the patient accounting application in a provider organization or the claims adjudication system in the health plan entity. The data elements captured in the provider claim—either an *institutional provider* (such as a hospital, nursing facility, home healthcare, outpatient surgery center, or hospice) or *professional provider*—include the items listed in Table 8.2 (Centers for Medicare and

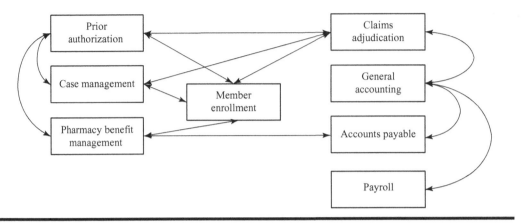

Figure 8.2 General relationships among health plan applications.

Medicaid Services, 2017). Often, medical claim data can be a comprehensive source of useful data for many operational performance analyses.

Claim data can be a useful start to an analysis project. However, that data will have limited value in associating clinical signs or symptoms with actual treatments or resource decisions. It also may not assist in identifying the

Table 8.2 Examples of Medical Claim Data Elements

Category	Examples
Patient demographics	Name, age, gender, address, ID number
Provider demographics	Provider name, address, ID number
Detail of fees billed	Units of service by hospital department or by procedure in professional claims
Diagnoses	Diagnoses described by ICD-10 diagnostic codes
Procedures	Procedures performed described by CPT code
Discharge status	Outcome of patient treatment—for example, discharged to home, discharged to nursing facility, transferred to other hospital, patient expired
Occurrences	For example, accident date, date therapy started, date of last menstrual period
Insurance	Insurance carrier name, policy number, data on subscriber if different from patient
Treating physician	Attending and consulting physician names and unique physician identification number

costs of resources used in treating a patient at a microlevel, such as the cost of implantable devices or the labor hours involved in one day of care in the intensive care unit. It is usually limited to identifying types of cases (e.g., by diagnosis or by insurer) or high-level comparisons of metrics by patient type, insurer, or treating physician. To associate clinical data with other types of data gathered in clinical applications, such as the EHR, database tools and some limited data manipulation skills will be needed.

Understanding and Managing Data

Administrative and clinical applications used in healthcare organizations rely on databases to compile and organize data for use within the application. A *database* is a collection of data organized in a series of *tables*, organized by type of data or subject, such as a listing of patients with date of birth or a table of medications used in a clinic. Each table is made up of multiple rows and columns, where each row is one *record* in the table and columns represent a *variable*. The databases of most contemporary health applications are organized in what is known as a *normalized database* form. A normalized database separates data into multiple different tables to minimize the duplication of items in the database. The normalized database relies on connections between tables using a common item, known as a *key*. An illustration of a simple normalized database for a physician clinic EHR is shown in Figure 8.3.

In this illustration, the patient, Fred Jones, was born on November 27, 1952; has Medicare insurance, policy number 40909Z; and was seen in the clinic on January 24, 2017, under encounter number 1583. The diagnosis was pancreatic cancer, and the service provided was an office visit for an established patient with a complex medical diagnosis. As you will note in Figure 8.3, getting all the information for the patient requires pulling elements from different tables in the EHR to obtain the variables that make up the details of this patient encounter. This normalized database helps information technology staff by minimizing the amount of storage space needed in computer hardware, but it presents a challenge to the manager wanting to analyze those data. The challenge arises from three different perspectives:

1. The manager must know how data are organized in the database to find all the various elements required to answer an analytical question.
2. The manager must understand the various keys used in the database to be able to join data elements from multiple tables in the database.

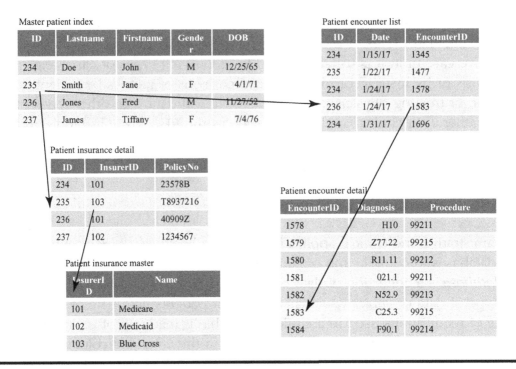

Figure 8.3   Illustration of normalized database.

3. The manager must have a database tool that can find the desired rows in the database table and join them with rows from other tables to create information that can answer a question such as "Which Medicare patients were seen in January with a diagnosis of pancreatic cancer?"—as was shown in this simple illustration.

Analytical Tools

The analytical tools that can be used to accomplish operational analyses can be as simple as a Microsoft Excel spreadsheet, where lists could be joined together using a simple combination of =VLOOKUP() functions to combine elements in two lists, such as that shown in Figure 8.4.

Note in Figure 8.4 how the patient ID in row 3, column A is used to find the patient encounter ID in the patient encounter table shaded in red. This approach using the Excel spreadsheet tool can be useful for simple analyses where joining few elements from small lists. Were this analysis to use much larger lists with more variables, the capacity of an Excel spreadsheet could be exceeded. That is where the analytical question may require a database query tool, such as Microsoft Access, Microsoft SQL Server, Oracle, or MySQL.

VLOOKUP ƒx =VLOOKUP($A3,$C$5:$E$18,3,FALSE)

ID	Lastname	Firstname	Gender	DOB	Encounter Date	EncounterID	Diagnosis	Procedure
236	Jones	Jones	Fred	M	1/24/17	$E$18,3,FALSE)	C25.3	99215

Master Pt Index

ID	Lastname	Firstname	Gender	DOB
234	Doe	John	M	12/25/65
235	Smith	Jane	F	4/1/71
236	Jones	Fred	M	11/27/52
237	James	Tiffany	F	7/4/76

Patient Encounter List

ID	Date	EncounterID
234	1/15/17	1345
235	1/22/17	1477
234	1/24/17	1578
236	1/24/17	1583
234	1/31/17	1696

Patient Encounter Detail

EncounterID	Diagnosis	Procedure
1578	H10	99211
1579	Z77.22	99215
1580	R11.11	99212

Figure 8.4 Simple Microsoft Excel join of two data tables.

Database tools such as those mentioned above use a *query* to find specific rows in a database table and join them with rows from other tables using one or more database keys. Such queries are often completed using a common database programming language like *Structured Query Language* (SQL). SQL can create queries that pick specific variables from tables, joining them based on one or more keys. The example given earlier of Mr. Jones might be carried out in SQL using a query such as this:

```
SELECT ID, Firstname, Lastname, DOB FROM MasterPatientIndex INNER
JOIN MasterPatientIndex.ID = PatientInsuranceDetail.ID,
InsurerID FROM
PatientInsuranceDetail, INNER JOIN MasterPatientIndex.ID =
PatientEncounterList.ID, PatientEncounterDetail.Diagnosis
INNER JOIN
PatientEncounterList.EncounterID = PatientEncounterDetail.
EncounterID,
Diagnosis from PatientEncounterDetail
WHERE PatientInsuranceDetail.InsurerID = "101" AND
PatientEncounterDetail.Diagnosis = "C25.3";
```

This SQL query would have sought out the first name, last name, date of birth, insurer ID code, and diagnosis code for all patients having Medicare insurance and a diagnosis of pancreatic cancer, just as was shown at the top of Figure 8.4. Thus, a database tool such as SQL can provide a great deal of analytical power to managers seeking data from the complex databases used in today's health applications. The details on application databases and the nuances of SQL programming needed to execute an analytical task like this are beyond the scope of this text. For more details on the composition of the application databases used in a healthcare organization, readers are encouraged to consult with their application vendor technical support teams. Many application vendors have help desk resources dedicated to providing managers with assistance on where to look for specific data elements or how to query application data tables. For more assistance on SQL query construction, the reader is encouraged to seek out an SQL programming resource, such as *Sam's Teach Yourself SQL in 24 Hours* by Stephens et al. (2015).

Analyzing Data

Database tools allow the manager to filter and combine large tables to complete very sophisticated queries that can create a very specific data set usable for detailed analysis of a management question or issue (Madsen, 2012). However, it is important to know about the nature of the data when designing an analytical project—are the variables numeric, alpha characters, or special codes using a combination of letters and numbers? Successful healthcare analytics requires an understanding of how the data are organized and what they express.

A good example of this challenge comes in the use of diagnosis and procedure codes in the EHR. Diagnoses and inpatient hospital surgeries are described using a combination of letters and numbers in the International Classification of Diseases, of which the tenth edition is currently in use in the United States (known as ICD-10). This coding set provides a very detailed description of diagnostic findings, using a code that varies from three to five characters in length, with or without a decimal point included (Sinha, 2013). The ICD-10 code for myocardial infarction (without other descriptive terms) is I21.3. However, that diagnosis could be further subdivided into the location of the infarction injury in the heart, such as the anterior (I21.09), inferior (I21.19), or lateral (I21.29) aspect of the myocardium. Similarly, a malignant cancer diagnosis in the colon is generally described by the ICD-10 code C18, but can be further subdivided based on the location along the colon by the cecum (C18.0), ascending colon (C18.2), transverse colon (C18.4), or descending colon (C18.6).

In the ICD-10 coding set, numbers and letters are used interchangeably, where numerals act as another letter. Numerals in this code set cannot be used for calculation. The key for the manager is to have resources that can assist in understanding this detailed code set and provide guidance in selecting the correct codes for the analytical project. Additional resources and training in the use of the ICD-10 coding system can be found through the American Health Information Management Association (www.ahima.org).

Procedures (other than inpatient surgeries) or other diagnostic or treatment services are described using the *Common Procedural Terminology* (CPT) code set. A CPT code is made up of five characters, and like the ICD-10 diagnosis code, can include both letters and numerals. CPT is subdivided into three broad categories. Category I procedures are those performed by healthcare providers for patients and are subdivided into six general subcategories:

1. Evaluation and management (codes 99201–99499)—Usually physician services that involve assessing the patient's medical history and current condition and rendering treatment or creating a treatment plan
2. Anesthesia (codes 00100–01999 and 99100–99140)—Specific to the type of anesthesia given and any additional services needed to safely administer anesthesia with other health conditions

3. Surgery (codes 10021–69990)—Provide a description of surgical procedures provided by the physician and the surgical facility and are organized by the area of the body where the surgery was performed;
4. Radiology (codes 70010–79999)—Describe any diagnostic imaging studies performed or any treatment procedures that used radiology services
   in addition (such as checking the placement of an implantable device
   using fluoroscopy)—this set of codes is organized by the type of imaging modality used, such as computerized tomography or ultrasound
5. Pathology and laboratory (80047–89398)—This range of codes describes
   diagnostic tests performed in the clinical laboratory, as well as any professional examination of patient tissue by a pathologist
6. Medicine (codes 90281–99199 and 99500–99607)—Describe all other
   nonsurgical treatment services rendered by a healthcare professional,
   and again are organized by the body system involved in the treatment
   (Sinha, 2013; MB&CC, n.d.)

Category II CPT codes are used to track services and quality of care
measures and are made up of four digits with an F at the end. These codes
are used in much the same way as a Category I code described above, but
are used for statistical tracking of preventive health services that are not
currently reimbursable by insurers. These codes are subdivided into nine
groups used to describe patient quality of care metrics:

1. Composite measures (CPT codes 0001F–0015F)—Address conditions
   that may impact the entire patient, such as code 0002F for assessment
   of a patient's tobacco use by smoking
2. Patient management (CPT codes 0500F–0575F)—Describe specific
   actions by a physician to manage an identified health condition, such as
   code 0556F for developing a plan of care to achieve control of elevated
   lipids in a patient
3. Patient history (CPT codes 1000F–1220F)—These codes further examine
   the presence of conditions reported by the patient in a medical history,
   such as code 1005F for evaluation of asthma symptoms
4. Physical examination (CPT codes 2000F–2050F)—This range of codes
   considers management of findings made during a physical exam, such
   as code 2044F, which documents a mental health assessment
5. Diagnostic and screening processes and results (CPT codes
   3006F–3573F)—These codes are used to document review of the results
   of previously ordered diagnostic tests, an example of which is CPT code

3015F, which is used to document review of the results of a cervical cancer screening test

6. Therapeutic, preventive, or other interventions (CPT codes 4000F–4306F)—This range of CPT codes documents the performance of other health treatments or interventions, such as code 4062F to document the referral of a patient for psychotherapy

7. Follow-up or other outcomes (CPT codes 5005F–5100F)—These codes describe actions by a treating professional to act on the results of treatment or physical exam, as done with CPT code 5020F to document the communication of a patient's treatment summary to another physician or health professional

8. Patient safety (CPT codes 6005F–6045F)—This set of codes describes actions taken by the treating provider to protect the patient's safety during treatment, such as with CPT code 6040F to document the use of radiation protection devices during a diagnostic imaging test or treatment

9. Structural measures (CPT codes 7010F–7025F)—This set of CPT codes documents actions by a treating provider to conduct follow-up with the patient on screening results as would be done using CPT code 7020F for evaluating a patient for mammography follow-up (MB&CC, n.d.)

Category III CPT codes encompass those used for new technologies, services, or procedures that do not yet have a permanent CPT code assigned to them. This classification of CPT code is like the Category II setup in that it is a five-character code using four digits followed by the letter T. These codes are usually used for data collection and tracking the utilization of emerging technologies or services. These procedures are often involved with biomedical research and have not yet been approved for use as a Category I procedure code. Updates to the Category I codes are published every other year by the American Medical Association.

CPT codes are further detailed using a set of two-character (letter or numeral) modifiers that provide an additional description of the service. A *modifier* is an adjunct to a CPT code that provides a further description of the service or procedure. One example is use of the modifier code 50 on a surgical procedure to show that the procedure was performed on both the left and right sides of the body. Other modifiers frequently used are those to describe the primary procedure done during a surgical case where more than one procedure was performed on the patient (modifier 51) or if multiple surgeons were involved in the case (modifier 62).

When examining data from a facility (e.g., a hospital or surgical center) patient billing system, the analytical task may require identification of the facility department that provided a service to the patient. A facility *revenue code* can be used to identify that department. The revenue code is a four-digit numeric code that shows the department a service was provided in. A list of common revenue codes is shown in Table 8.3 (Centers for Medicare and Medicaid Services, 2017).

Table 8.3   Examples of Facility Revenue Codes

Revenue Code	Department Name
0111	Room and board—private—medical/surgical/GYN
0121	Room and board—semiprivate—medical/surgical/GYN
0200	Intensive care unit
0210	Coronary care unit
0250	Pharmacy
0260	IV therapy
0270	Medical/surgical supplies
0300	Laboratory
0310	Pathology
0320	Diagnostic radiology
0340	Nuclear medicine
0350	CT scan
0360	Surgical services
0370	Anesthesia
0380	Blood and blood products
0410	Respiratory care
0420	Physical therapy
0430	Occupational therapy
0450	Emergency room
0490	Ambulatory surgery
0510	Outpatient clinic

(Continued)

Table 8.3 (Continued) Examples of Facility Revenue Codes

Revenue Code	Department Name
0550	Skilled nursing
0610	Magnetic resonance imaging
0630	Special medications requiring detailed coding—usually high-cost medications
0650	Hospice
0710	Recovery room
0720	Labor and delivery
0730	EKG/ECG
0780	Telemedicine
0800	Inpatient Renal Dialysis
0820	Outpatient hemodialysis
0900	Behavioral health services
0990	Patient convenience items
1000	Behavioral health accommodation (e.g., residential treatment or group home)
2100	Alternative therapies (e.g., acupuncture, massage, and reflexology)
3100	Adult care

Many analytic questions may involve the use of medications, which can vary by manufacturer, name, and packaging (Langabeer and Helton, 2016). Attempting to screen medication data by name and then these other characteristics could be very challenging were it not for a standardized system of identifying patient medications—the *National Drug Code* (NDC). The NDC is a 10-digit unique identifier that allows an analysis to focus on specific characteristics of medications—manufacturer, drug name, and packaging type. The NDC is broken into three segments:

1. *Manufacturer*: Identified by a five-digit code, such as 666582 for Merck
2. *Product*: Identified by a three-digit code, such as 311 for Vytorin, 10 mg tablet
3. *Packaging*: Identified by a two-digit code, such as 31 for 30 tablets in one bottle (Langabeer and Helton, 2016)

This section has elaborated only a few of the myriad coding sets available in healthcare computer applications. The ones described here are among the more common and are often used across multiple applications. This knowledge can help the design of an analytical project by directing the manager to where data can be found, how data are captured, and how they are organized within the healthcare application he or she is seeking data from. It is important to realize that much of the data stored in healthcare applications is set up in a coded structure like described here. Healthcare analysis projects usually cannot be answered with a simple list of diagnoses or procedures but must be translated into the coding structure used by our data gathering tools. However, the level of detail with which data can be gathered now using electronic applications can be of significant help in addressing some of today's questions concerning quality of patient care, preventive health interventions, the volume and nature of services used by healthcare providers, and the costs of care for patients.

Statistical Analysis in Health Analytics

Once a manager has access to data relevant to the analytic project, the next step is to analyze the data to find answers to help improve operational efficiency, quality of care performance, or utilization of resources. Usually, this is done through statistical analysis. There are many ways in which a statistical analysis can be completed, and most of them will be beyond the scope of this text. However, a statistical analysis does not have to be highly sophisticated to yield meaningful information to managers. Much can be learned through simple descriptive statistics and measures of central tendency (Thurman, 2008).

Consider an analysis of the costs of treating a Medicare patient with pneumonia in a hospital, comparing six different physicians over the course of one year. Data for such an example analysis are presented in Table 8.4. The data gathered here could come from multiple sources, including the electronic medical record; the patient accounting system; and pharmacy, lab, and radiology systems—all joined together through patient identification numbers in the MPI, which connects patient-specific data across these different applications. The data in Table 8.4 include a unique identifier for the treating physician; the number of discharges by that physician; the number of inpatient days for all that physician's cases with that diagnosis; the total costs for pharmacy, laboratory services, and radiology services; the number

Table 8.4 Example Analysis Data

Physician	Discharge	Days	Rx Cost ($)	Lab Cost ($)	Radiology Cost ($)	Discharge Home	Discharge to SNF	Expired	Readmits
A	61	244	64,896	77,092	51,964	29	29	3	5
B	53	269	63,195	55,416	44,911	23	22	7	0
C	30	157	41,600	45,020	48,802	14	10	6	3
D	46	232	54,270	65,770	39,550	25	18	2	4
E	95	579	134,420	108,420	84,216	50	43	2	12
F	12	87	31,376	27,344	28,424	5	6	1	0

Note: SNF, skilled nursing facility.

of patients discharged directly to home; the number of patients discharged to skilled nursing; the number of patients who died in the hospital; and the number of patients readmitted within 30 days of discharge for the same condition. This list could be further condensed by identifying only those cases discharged with a diagnosis of pneumonia and insured by Medicare. With just this simple data listing, managers can gain significant insights to potential areas to improve outcomes, costs of care, and therefore the overall performance of the organization.

Since Medicare reimburses hospitals on a fixed payment per discharge, this analysis should seek out opportunities to reduce costs and reduce the length of stay per discharge. In addition, under the ACA hospitals are penalized by Medicare if a patient is readmitted for the same condition within 30 days of discharge. So, it should also look to minimize the rate of readmissions, both to minimize financial penalties and improve patient outcomes. With that backdrop, hospital managers can make great insights into pneumonia care with only a few calculations.

Descriptive statistics usually involve a *mean* (average for a variable), median (middle point of all values for that variable), *standard deviation* (measures how "scattered" the values are for that variable), and *coefficient of variation* (how much the data are scattered, relative to the mean). Also, note the minimum and maximum observed values and the difference between those values—known as the *range*. Since each physician has multiple cases, the analysis should start with calculating the average length of stay per discharge (patient days divided by the number of discharges), pharmacy cost per discharge, lab cost per discharge, and radiology cost per discharge for each physician. Then calculate the mean, median, and standard deviation of those costs per discharge for the pharmacy, lab, and radiology—as well as for the average length of stay. Mortality rates and readmission rates would also be helpful in assessing quality outcomes and so should be included in the analysis. Once data for the analysis have been gathered from the databases of applications used in the organization, they can be transferred to an Excel spreadsheet for easy calculation of these statistical measures using the Excel functions described in Table 8.5.

The calculations for this analysis are shown in Table 8.6.

Reviewing these calculations will show some meaningful insights to pneumonia care in the hospital. The cost per discharge data show limited variability with coefficients of variation, with all at or below about 0.50. When considering that physician F is much higher than all other physicians

Table 8.5   Excel Functions to Calculate Statistical Measures

Statistical Measure	Excel Function
Mean	= AVERAGE(range of cells)
Median	= MEDIAN(range of cells)
Standard deviation	= STDEV(range of cells)
Coefficient of variation	No function—calculate as standard deviation/mean
Minimum value	= MIN(range of cells)
Maximum value	= MAX(range of cells)
Range	No function—calculate by subtracting the minimum value from the maximum value

in the cost metrics, the data appear fairly concentrated around the means. This limited variability tells the manager that the cost patterns among physicians A through E are fairly consistent. Similarly, the length of stay is not widely distributed, especially when considering that, again, physician F is much higher than the mean for the group.

The readmission rate overall is high, at a mean of 7%, ranging from 0% for physician F to a high of 13% for physician E. Considering that for each readmission the hospital is penalized the amount it would have been paid for the admission (essentially providing care in the second admission without payment), that is a significant problem requiring further investigation. Similarly, the analysis also shows that on average, 1 in 11 (9%) Medicare patients treated for pneumonia died while hospitalized—a rate significantly higher than the national average of 3.3% (Centers for Disease Control and Prevention, 2017). Both observations should warrant further investigation. Some guidance may come from looking at the work done by physician E, whose death rate is lower than average for the other physicians in the hospital and low than the national average.

With respect to the costs of care for these physicians, the lowest overall cost of care was observed with physician B, driven primarily by having the lowest lab and radiology costs per discharge and the second lowest pharmacy cost per discharge. Interestingly, this physician also had the third lowest average length of stay and the lowest readmission rate among the staff caring for pneumonia cases in the hospital. Conversely, the hospital may

Table 8.6   Calculation of Statistics by Physician for Pneumonia Care

Physician	ALOS	Rx/Discharge	Lab/Discharge	Radiology/Discharge	Total/Discharge	Mortality	Readmit
A	4.0	$1063.87	$1263.80	$851.87	$3179.54	5%	8%
B	5.1	$1192.36	$1045.58	$847.36	$3085.30	14%	0%
C	5.2	$1386.67	$1500.67	$1626.67	$4514.01	21%	10%
D	5.0	$1179.78	$1429.78	$859.78	$3469.35	5%	9%
E	6.1	$1414.95	$1141.26	$886.48	$3442.69	2%	13%
F	7.3	$2614.67	$2278.67	$2368.67	$7262.01	9%	0%
Mean	5.45	$1475.38	$1443.26	$1240.14	$4158.81	9%	7%
Median	5.15	$1289.51	$1346.79	$873.13	$3456.02	7%	8%
SD	1.11	573.81	443.38	632.10	1603.47	0.07	0.05
CV	0.20	0.39	0.31	0.50	0.39	0.75	0.81
Min	4.0	$1063.87	$1045.58	$847.36	$3085.30	2%	0%
Max	7.3	$2614.67	$2278.67	$2368.67	$7262.01	21%	13%
Range	3.3	$1550.80	$1233.08	$1521.31	$4176.69	19%	13%

Note: ALOS, average length of stay; SD, standard deviation; CV, coefficient of variation.

have a cost problem with physician F, where costs per discharge in all three departments and in length of stay are all far above the mean for the group. Management may have lessons to share among the physicians in the hospital by further examination of how physician B manages the care of pneumonia patients.

While a table of variables with calculated statistics may be useful to managers, supplementing that work with a graph may help to visualize some of the relationships observed in the analysis. A bar graph of the average cost per discharge metrics used in this analysis is shown in Figure 8.5.

Applying Analytics in Performance Improvement

The tools described earlier in this chapter can be applied to performance improvement in healthcare organizations. Performance improvement tools include performance dashboards, measurement of value-based purchasing performance metrics, and applying focused analysis to Lean or Six Sigma quality improvement projects.

The use of a dashboard can help to put specific performance metrics in an "at a glance" format that makes it easy for managers to monitor and trend

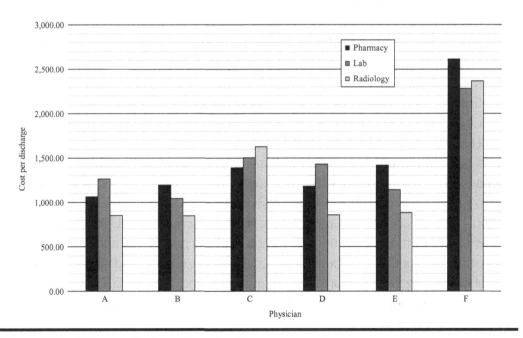

Figure 8.5   Cost per discharge by physician.

calculated values for those metrics. To develop performance metrics, management should follow these steps:

1. Define the measurement and specific data elements to be used in calculating the performance metrics.
2. Establish any criteria for including or excluding data needed to develop a performance baseline that will be used to determine if a metric is in or out of standard for the organization.
3. Define the data gathering approach needed not only to establish the baseline value but also to monitor ongoing performance against that metric.
4. Establish the desired outcome to be measured by that metric, such as improving the compliance with a value-based purchasing objective (Langabeer and Helton, 2016).

Once these metrics have been established, management should review them to be sure that measurement of these metrics will in fact lead to the desired change in organizational performance. Frequency of measurement is an important decision to be made in creating a performance dashboard using analytic results. The reporting should be frequent enough to alert management to unfavorable trends, but not be so frequent as to create information overload with management and prevent them from seeing unfavorable trends. In addition, greater frequency of reporting will require greater resources to be devoted to the analytics function to create more report data—and such resource commitments may be greater than the benefits to be reaped. Management must therefore make a reasoned estimate of how much information should be generated on what frequency to gain benefit without excessive commitment of resources to performance measuring analytics (Langabeer and Helton, 2016).

It is also important to establish metrics that can be influenced by management action. Tracking metrics that managers are not able to control will simply lead to managers ignoring reported observations. It can also lead to frustration, burnout, and loss of management talent by the organization. Understanding the data available to the organization for analytical purposes will allow managers to identify metrics that can be influenced by management and allow greater control of organization performance (Langabeer and Helton, 2016).

Examples of metrics that would align with value-based purchasing objectives include items such as

- Administration of aspirin to all patients presenting in the emergency room with signs of a myocardial infarction
- Measurement of the number of cases where patients are given prophylactic antibiotics for surgery
- Identification of patients having adverse medication reactions
- Measurement of readmission rates by diagnosis

Using the first example given in this chapter, a dashboard may include measurement of operating costs per surgical case by physician, as illustrated earlier, to monitor possible opportunities to improve costs of care. A simple analysis like the one described in this chapter, where costs by department were profiled by physician, could have provided Mr. Rogers with data that would have allowed him to proactively address this challenge and prevent financial losses coming from a newly recruited medical staff member. In the second scenario, Ms. James could have had a routine report generated from her claims adjudication system that would have perhaps profiled CPT codes paid by physician and compared the frequency of payment of those codes among all providers, and allowed her to note a potentially fraudulent trend in billing and refer it for further investigation.

Summary

Analytics in healthcare businesses can provide powerful information about how organization performance is and how it could be improved. Healthcare organizations gather tremendous amounts of data that can be used to further the analysis of operational performance and identify areas of weakness. However, it has only been in recent years that these organizations have routinely gathered data in a format that can be readily analyzed.

While data gathered in healthcare organizations are now digitized to a large extent, additional effort is needed to integrate disparate data sources together into a meaningful whole. However, there are logical connections among these data elements that can allow these analytic tasks to be quite fruitful. The organization does not need a high degree of sophistication in statistical analysis to generate meaningful information that is usable to improve performance.

Key Terms

Structured data, unstructured data, analytics, electronic medical record, electronic health record, clinical data, administrative data, master patient index, institutional provider, professional provider, database, table, variable, normalized database, key, query, SQL, ICD-10, CPT, modifier, revenue code, National Drug Code (NDC), mean, median, standard deviation, coefficient of variation

Discussion Questions

1. What is the difference in analytical techniques that can be used for structured versus unstructured data?
2. What are the reasons why healthcare has not embraced greater use of analytics until recently?
3. What role does an MPI have in other databases and systems in an organization?

References

Centers for Disease Control and Prevention (2017). Trends in inpatient hospital deaths: National Hospital Discharge Survey. Available at https://www.cdc.gov/nchs/products/databriefs/db118.htm.

Centers for Medicare and Medicaid Services (2017). Medicare Claims Processing Manual. Available at https://www.cms.gov/Regulations-and-Guidance/Guidance/Manuals/Internet-Only-Manuals-IOMs-Items/CMS018912.html?DLPage=1&DLEntries=10&DLSort=0&DLSortDir=ascending.

Glandon G, Slovensky D, and Smaltz D (2013). *Information Systems for Healthcare Management*. 8th edn. Chicago: Health Administration Press.

Hoyt R and Yoshihashi A (2014). *Health Informatics: Practical Guide for Healthcare and Information Technology Professionals*. 6th edn. Pensacola, FL: Informatics Education.

MB&CC (n.d.). Intro to CPT coding. Available at http://www.medicalbillingandcoding.org/intro-to-cpt/.

Kaiser Family Foundation (2013). Summary of the Affordable Care Act. Available at http://www.kff.org/health-reform/fact-sheet/summary-of-the-affordable-care-act/.

Kaiser Family Foundation (2017). How much is health spending expected to grow? Available at http://www.healthsystemtracker.org/chart-collection/much-health-spending-expected-grow/?_sft_category=spending.

Langabeer J and Helton J (2016). *Healthcare Operations Management—A Systems Perspective*. 2nd edn. Burlington, MA: Jones & Bartlett.

Madsen L (2012). *Healthcare Business Intelligence: A Guide to Empowering Successful Data Reporting and Analytics*. Hoboken, NJ: Wiley.

Sinha P (2013). *Electronic Health Records: Standards, Coding Systems, Frameworks, and Infrastructures*. Hoboken, NJ: Wiley.

Stephens R, Jones A, and Plew R (2015). *Sam's Teach Yourself SQL in 24 Hours*. 6th edn. Washington, DC: Pearson Education.

Strome T (2013). *Healthcare Analytics for Quality and Performance Improvement*. Hoboken, NJ: Wiley.

Thurman P (2008). *MBA Fundamentals Statistics*. New York: Kaplan Publishing.

Wager K, Lee F, and Glaser J (2013). *Health Care Information Systems: A Practical Approach for Health Care Management*. 3rd edn. Hackensack, NJ: Wiley.

Chapter 9

Population Health Management

Bobbie Kite

Contents

Quality is not an act, it is a habit.

Aristotle
Philosopher

Introduction

Population health is one of the more common buzzwords in recent years. Understanding *population health management* (PHM) will be useful for quality and performance improvement analysts in years to come. A useful discussion surrounding population health requires an understanding of its roots in public health and evolution to a focus on information technology (IT) and data. The growth of PHM over the last 15 years means that it developed into its own healthcare delivery perspective. In this chapter, we propose that four perspectives include patient, provider, payer, and population (4Ps). These different perspectives, or lenses, frame how analysts view the healthcare delivery system. This chapter describes the 4Ps and discusses how PHM and analytics impact performance improvement. As healthcare organizations navigate through performance improvement cycles, this leads to changes in population health. In this chapter, we review literature and themes surrounding population health, explore its unique place as a healthcare delivery perspective, articulate its public health and data components, and explore population health improvement strategies.

What Is Population Health?

There are differing themes surrounding population health, but a commonly accepted definition was proposed by Kindig and Stoddart in 2003 as "the health outcomes of a group of individuals, including the distribution of such outcomes of the group." In breaking this down, they proposed that population health has three main components: health outcomes, patterns of health determinants, and policies and interventions, which we will explore further along in the chapter. The central idea is that the application of these components together would increase health equity and reduce health disparities caused by the negative effects of health factors for specific populations (Kindig and Stoddart, 2003). The reality is that the evolution of population health led us to a host of definitions that now extend beyond the traditional one (Kindig, 2015). These populations may now be based on factors such as diagnoses, clinical treatments, environmental factors, or specific sets of health factors. Simply stated, population health is a shift of focus from the health, health impact factors, and healthcare delivery circumstances of the individual to the health, health impact, and healthcare delivery circumstances of populations.

Many healthcare organizations have a difficult time understanding population health. A fair amount of this misunderstanding is due to its overlap with public health. Population health can be viewed as a juncture between the clinical care for subpopulations and the process of providing resources necessary for the public good. The Institute of Medicine (IOM) referred to this juncture as the Jacobson and Teutsch critique of population health as "total population health." The shift of population health toward clinical subpopulations may strengthen public health initiatives by utilizing varying interventions toward changing patterns of disease, healthcare delivery experiences, and costs. This process is referred to as PHM.

A common theme amid explanations of population health is a focus on IT, data, and analytics. The idea is that effective management of population health uses clinical, operational, behavioral, and billing data from varying organizations and entities that are in, or closely related to, the healthcare industry. This combination of treatment across specific populations helps determine the best value for population-wide interventions aimed at benefitting the individual, as well as the group. In theory, this process leads to improved population outcomes over time. Increasingly, population health is becoming a critical element of healthcare organizational performance improvement since the strategies determining outcomes between the two processes overlap (Kassler et al., 2017).

Measures of Population Health Status

As the healthcare industry changes, so does population health, but how do we measure those changes? Well, the measures are as varied as the range of interventions and programs (Chan et al., 2016). In addition to these varying measures, there are also clinical outcome measures related to disease-specific population health programs. Therefore, many population health measures are paralleled with clinical quality measures. While clinical quality measures tend to be centered on cost and patient quality of life, population health measures differ in that they should be able to

- Transform individual clinical data points to information for external parties
- Account for the health status of unseen patients within the primary organization
- Integrate community public health initiatives
- Include social, behavioral, and environmental factors of the population
- Incorporate health-related quality of life

A recent domain analysis revealed that more than 2,200 quality measures were related to population health. These measures were divided into 6 domain categories and 22 topic areas (Kassler et al., 2017). These domains ranged from health behavior measures, which represented the largest domain, to community and collaboration measures, which represented the smallest of the domains. So, our choices for utilizing and developing measures are far reaching.

Population health measures heavily focus on life expectancy (LE) as it relates to quality of life indicators (Chan et al., 2016). The thinking here is that LE as an indication of quality may be misleading without a sound definition of what longer life means. For example, there may be an intervention that enables people to live longer, but they may be living longer in poor health and therefore not really improving the population's health. For this reason, more specific population health measures related to LE have been developed. Some examples of population aging measures include disability by demographic factors, remaining LE, public pension age, and handgrip strength. This research focused on taking a traditional chronological age measure and modifying it into multiple, more specific, measures to account for changing characteristics of growing older. These metrics were then converted to a common "alpha-age" metric and used to predict outcomes. New combined alpha-age population health metrics did a better job predicting than the simple physical measures. Although this example is specific to age, the process of characteristic approaches can be used to develop other population health measures in a similar manner. While these are research-based specific measures, the takeaway here is to understand the diversity and complexity of your options when establishing population health status measures.

Interaction with Community Public Health Service Providers

Since we are aware of the overlap between population health and public health, it's important to determine the relevant stakeholders that should be, or already are, involved with initiatives. *Stakeholders* are those who are internally and externally interested in your organization's initiatives. A crucial part in long-term success of population health programs may be external stakeholders, such as public health entities that provide services the organization might not otherwise have. These entities can also provide expertise related to health factors in the populations of interest. By including pertinent community public health entities, you open the way for the cocreation of measures and the direction you want to move toward with your PHM initiatives.

For example, population health programs that focus on providing mental health interventions may span several clinical public and private healthcare organizations. These programs may be successful on outcomes such as screening rates of disease, but may be hard-pressed to demonstrate improvement related to typical outcome measures for intervention programs, such as reduced hospital readmissions or improved clinical outcomes. By collaborating with public health entities, measures can be created to monitor the change of distribution of outcomes within a group toward increasing health equity. These may be centered on the health literacy levels of identified stakeholders, such as community and healthcare organizational leaders, or on standardizing policies to support both individuals and independent healthcare organizations within the community.

In our example above related to mental health interventions, municipal housing coalitions could better serve the community if they were informed about the programs that your healthcare organization offered. This information would allow them to provide expertise concerning nonclinical measures related to mental health areas, such as homelessness, domestic violence, and crime rates. The scope of the population health program would then span across both clinical and public resources to affect change for the subgroup of those affected by mental health issues in the community. This interaction could be used across any type of population health initiative. The key takeaway here is to determine the possible public health overlap of your initiatives and then explore how this interaction can increase the success of initiatives. It is also important to bring internal stakeholders to the table to discuss how these external stakeholder interactions could further organizational performance improvement initiatives.

Now, let's articulate the steps involved when interacting with community public health services regarding a population health initiative.

- *Identify internal and external stakeholders*: Once you articulate the population health issue you'd like to provide a program for, connect the IT, operations, and senior leadership of your organization to make sure everyone is aware of the initiative. This is a good time to gauge your organization's willingness and ability to align leadership and share goals with outside public health entities. Next, conduct research at city, county, regional, and state levels to identify relevant public health entities playing in the space. See what academic partnerships exist and investigate any current or future plans for population health interventions to address the issue. Compile a list of these efforts and the questions they are seeking to answer, and then reengage your internal stakeholders for feedback and reassess their willingness to align leadership and share goals concerning an initiative before beginning to meet with the entities.
- *Meet with community public health entities*: Contact and meet with the entities to discuss their current initiatives. Keep things simple, and keep your agenda about learning from them instead of simply informing them of what your organization wants to do. When you find out about other initiatives, determine the ability to build a bridge with their efforts and gauge their willingness to align leadership and share goals in your initiative. Academic partners can sometimes make this process easier since they represent a neutral party, in theory.

■ *Planning*: Work with internal and external stakeholders to develop a conceptual model of what you are proposing, and then work in unison to build mutually beneficial outcome measures. Draft a plan to operationalize and evaluate the initiative, and use internal stakeholders to ensure alignment with organizational performance improvement efforts. Make your rounds with external stakeholders once more to ensure buy-in.

■ *Making things work*: Use departmental and organizational champions to get the initiative moving and keep stakeholders engaged and communicating. Follow the operational plan, and stay flexible to modifications when necessary. Be aware of the common language being built among stakeholders, and pay close attention to opportunities to gather program data across stakeholders.

■ *Outcomes and sustainability*: Evaluate your initiative and make sure you create a feedback loop to your stakeholders answering their original questions. The sustainability of your efforts depends in large part on the perceived value of interaction between the organization and public health entities, as well as how well initiative outcomes align with performance improvement efforts. Ultimately, the interaction here can create a powerful story about lessons learned and lay the foundation for future population health initiatives for stakeholders.

Factors Influencing Population Health Status

Population health status is influenced by five major categories of factors, or *determinants of health*: genetics, health behaviors, healthcare, social environment, and physical environment. Figure 9.1 illustrates the percentage these factors are estimated to contribute to early death (Schroeder, 2007).

Genetic factors are biological in nature and may include inheritance and the likelihood of developing disease. Health behavior factors may include drug use, diet and nutrition, and exercise patterns. Healthcare factors relate to items such as access, cost, quality, and continuity of care. Social environment factors include items such as education level, occupation, income brackets, and social support networks. Lastly, physical environment factors may include soil, air, water quality, and workplaces. Therefore, if you want to affect changes in outcomes, program initiatives should be designed to influence one or more of these areas.

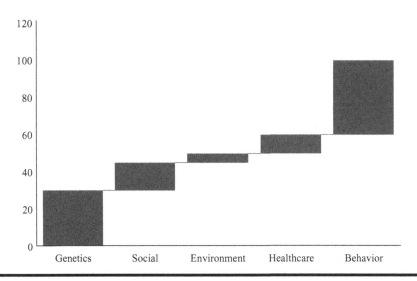

Figure 9.1   Determinants of health and contribution to early death.

Impact of Health Disparities and Inequities

As you design population health initiatives, it's important to understand not only determinants of health, but also how the outcomes of these are affected by health disparities and inequities. For instance, you may roll out a program to increase the health of the population centered on a disease. If there are subgroups who have an increased likelihood of developing the disease, then you would have a *health disparity* between subgroups and your program's effectiveness would be affected by this. You might then want to reduce the difference in rates of this disease between one subgroup and another to decrease differences in outcomes for these subgroups. Think of health disparities as the difference between subgroups stemming from (but not limited to) racial and ethnic differences (Kindig, 2015). From a broader perspective, research regarding upstream factors of health related to social and physical environments requires organizations to apply programs in broad ways. This means that planning and analyses may need to be conceptualized in nontraditional ways. Simply stated, there are five main categories of factors or determinants of health that can be intervened on, but the level of outcome change is affected by the amount of disparity that exists in the original population.

Now that we've explored disparity, let's examine inequity. Where health disparity is concerned with equality related to the amounts of a factor distributed between groups, equity is concerned with the amount of what is equal being appropriate for the group. For example, everybody in a group may get the same meal, but that doesn't mean it's enough for the various caloric needs in the group. You can think of *health inequity* as being avoidable or preventable health outcomes.

To help align your population health and performance improvement initiatives, it might be helpful to use reports such as "Healthy People 2020" and "CDC Health Disparities and Inequalities Report" (CHDIR). The "Healthy People 2020" report focuses on more general concepts, while the CHDIR has detailed research data and reports related to disparities. These reports are a concrete place to begin looking for initiatives that would lead to improved population health outcomes, as well as align with an organization's overall mission and goals.

Healthcare Delivery Systems and the 4Ps

Now that we've had a thorough review of the literature and themes surrounding population health, we can move into the application of PHM within the healthcare delivery system. The *healthcare delivery system* is the interaction of different healthcare organizations working together in the healthcare space. This term can be used to refer to healthcare delivery organizations across the entire United States, or it can refer to healthcare organizations working together in a specific area. For this chapter, we refer to the nationwide concept of a single healthcare delivery system. We will use the 4Ps as a framework for the discussion of PHM within the healthcare delivery system.

The 4Ps are lenses through which each of these perspective groups experience the health industry itself and those industries that are outside of the health industry, but are in some way related (in this chapter, the word *industry* is used to refer to this relationship). This includes its services, products, processes, and health delivery systems. A perspective can have multiple lenses for different groups, but each of the four major perspectives has a set of general characteristics that summarizes the perspective's ability to influence population health. It's important to remember that organizations can see the industry from different perspectives, but each organization still has one dominant lens to view the industry from. For example, although a commercial health insurance company might offer health coaching services, which would be seen through the provider perspective, most of their member base is looking to them to pay the medical bills. This means they are primarily seeing the industry through the payer perspective lens. Now that we have a base understanding of the 4Ps, let's explore them further.

How do these four perspectives relate to the cycle of population health? While each group, or organization, views the industry from its dominant perspective, it is a part of the industry as well. So, while the viewpoint of each organization is somewhat singular, the way organizations inside the industry are seen from the outside is plural. As groups from each perspective organize their own efforts, or unintentionally position population health initiatives, the effects ripple through the industry in the form of population health outcomes. In this way, the 4Ps perspectives inform the capabilities of organizations and groups to affect population health. If the goal is to increase capacity for population health, then combining efforts across perspectives through the pooling of resources is a workable solution. Figure 9.2 provides a visual representation of this cycle.

The 4Ps framework also works well when thinking in terms of performance improvement because the inputs and results that are being transformed differ based on the overall perspective of the organization. For example, the population health and performance improvement initiatives that a typical provider organization, such as a community hospital, might pursue would be very different from those of a consumer company, like Garmin. There are general characteristics, like scope of services and quality measures, that will be consistent for the perspectives. In this way, the perspectives can act as guidelines for both population health and performance

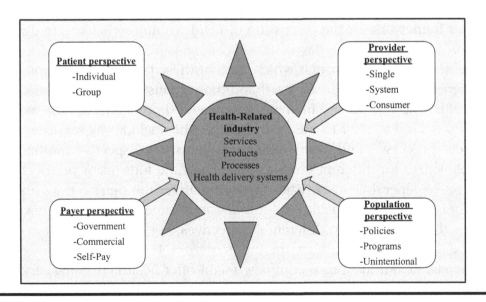

Figure 9.2   4Ps and population health cycle.

improvement initiatives. The 4Ps are not mutually exclusive by any means, but are meant to act as a beginning context for discussion. For example, the community hospital is seen from the patient perspective when viewed within the industry, but views the industry itself from the provider perspective. While both perspectives exist in relation to the community hospital, the provider perspective lens is dominant since this perspective dictates what performance improvement initiatives are relevant and possible.

When we think about population health from this point forward, we are really thinking more in terms of PHM, since this refers to the iterative process of programs aimed at improving outcomes, experiences, and costs (Kindig, 2015). Figure 9.3 illustrates this cycle and the general components involved. It begins with having members of a healthcare organization, along with operational and nonoperational data (more on this later in the chapter). This combination is then mixed with whatever population health program is chosen, and leads to improved population health measures. In theory, this equation leads to improved outcomes, experiences, and costs. What's portrayed here is a best-case scenario, but the key takeaway is that whatever the result, modifications will always need to be made before the next iteration of the cycle.

We have now set the stage to look at PHM and performance improvement through the 4Ps framework. Again, it's imperative to remember that although organizations can be viewed from the lens of more than one

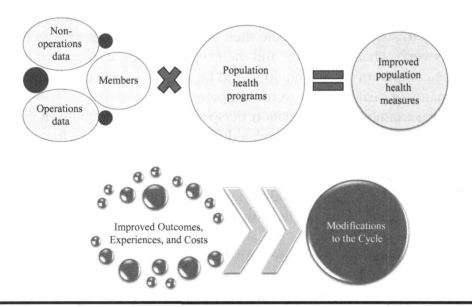

Figure 9.3 Population health improvement.

perspective, each organization has a dominant perspective that describes the lens through with its members see the industry, including its service, products, delivery processes, and health delivery systems. Next, we explore continuum of care, care coordination, and network affiliation strategies as they relate to PHM, performance improvement, and the 4Ps.

Continuum of Care

A *continuum of care*, in its simplest form, is the range of a patient's (or consumer's) healthcare. It's important to note that population health sits on the two ends of a continuum of care. It spans from self-care, in the form of exercising and other wellness activities, to inpatient care. You can also think of the continuum of care in terms of a time horizon. It's the path that someone, or a group of people, follow to receive the care they need. As you can imagine, there are considerable gaps in this continuum for some people. We can think about this continuum, population health, and performance improvement as an opportunity to combine efforts and reduce duplication of resources. Let's explore the continuum from the 4Ps framework.

We begin with the patient perspective. This is how a patient or con-sumer or a group of patients or consumers sees their ability to get the care they need across differing levels of wellness or sickness. Cost of services, availability of services, and range of services, both within and outside of a health system, are part of their continuum of care. What items might affect their ability to successfully navigate their continuum? Factors such as money, social network, where they live, and their type of medical insurance all affect the continuum (these should sound familiar from when we covered determinants of health earlier in the chapter).

Next, we examine the population perspective. The continuum of care here might be affected by policy related to clean water and air. It could also be related to larger programs, such Life's Simple Seven by the American Heart Association. The patient perspective is concerned with ensuring that people and groups can stay healthy in general, while the population per-spective is to increase the public's awareness of items that affect their con-tinuum of care.

The provider perspective is perhaps the most complicated of the con-tinuum of care. There are three main scenarios of this perspective that might play out. The first involves organizations whose patients or consum-ers experience their product or service being delivered without a third party involved. You can think of these as providing direct interaction between a patient or consumer and a health product or service. This can be a positive interaction in terms of population health because the service is readily available to everyone (in theory). We should still be conscious of barriers, such as cost and access. An example of this is how Garmin, Apple, Google, and Samsung produce wearables to help track individual fitness. These companies produce devices that help facilitate population health change. The second scenario involves a single-organization clinical provider. Its patient or consumer base is primarily bound by payment structures that work with differing insurance configurations. This scenario also involves a smaller scope, since one organization is providing one main product or service. An example of this is a rural area primary care office. The third scenario involves a healthcare system providing clinical care. Their patient or consumer base also has multiple insurance configurations binding payment. Providing a larger continuum of care for patients or consumers is their strong suit. The major difference between these three scenarios and the continuum of care is the ability of these providers to track patient activity. If you think through the examples, which organization had the most complete picture of care that a patient or consumer experiences? The larger health system, right? Yes, but does that mean the patient or consumer automatically has a better continuum of care? This is a good question, and we will explore the answer a little later when we discuss value-based payment structures.

Finally, we have the payer perspective. This includes government payers like Medicaid and Medicare; private insurance companies like UnitedHealth, Aetna, and Blue Cross; and people who self-pay outside of insurance configurations. Since these groups pay the bills, they have the ability to see all patient patterns of care and care interactions along the continuum, right? Theoretically, yes, but groups that self-pay may not have the ability to track their claims as easily as government and commercial payers.

Now that we've explored the continuum of care from these different perspectives, what is the opportunity for population health? First, by closing the gaps in patient or consumer continuums of care, we gain the opportunity for larger groups of people to get the care they need and stay healthier for longer. Second, these gaps in the continuum represent opportunities for organizational improvement. Toward these aims, care coordination is a common solution to "fill the gaps" that connects with population health and performance improvement.

Care Coordination

Care coordination is the managing of care activities between and across industry services for individuals and groups. What does care coordination mean for population health? From the patient perspective, it means patients and consumers exploring their ability to use provider companies' and organizations' services and products, population-based tools, and payer resources to coordinate their own care. As they become vested in their own continuum of care, they become empowered and their health literacy increases (Reidy et al., 2017). From the provider perspective, it means these provider organizations and companies are able to either intentionally execute population health programs or unintentionally affect population health through care coordination programs and initiatives. Providers can work together to offer patients and consumers better options for coordinating their care. It's important to note that while health systems may have an easier time coordinating care because single clinical providers may be seen as outsiders to the main healthcare industry, this could be flipped to an advantage for single clinical providers. They may be easier to work with for smaller consumer-based companies. From the payer perspective, it means the largest opportunity for coordination of care. Since they have the most complete picture of where their patients or consumers go, they can look at individual, as well as subgroup, patterns. They can collaborate with providers, other payers, and/or population-based healthcare organizations to offer services to patients to coordinate care somewhat directly. In this case, while they have great capacity to discover population patterns and help with coordination, there must be trust between patients or participants, the payer organizations, and the providers. From the population perspective, it means policy and programs meant to help with funding, government mandates, and health literacy meant to aid in the process of care coordination.

What does care coordination mean for performance improvement? It means that from the provider perspective specifically, these organizations probably track clinical measures, and care coordination will likely improve their inputs, processes, and outcomes. While the payer and population perspectives may not track clinical measures, there are many other types of performance improvement measures that can be paralleled with care coordination efforts.

Network Affiliation Strategies

When we think of PHM, it's critical to think in terms of network affiliations. *Network affiliations* are when organizations work together to build affiliations and relationships. Whether we are focusing on continuums of care or care coordination, and regardless of perspective, relationships through networks are necessary for the short- and long-term success of PHM initiatives. There are several strategies organizations from different perspectives can use to develop these network connections.

For example, organizations selling directly to consumers or patients might be focused on items such as wearable devices or health coaching services, but this focus can be of benefit in building relationships across multiple health systems since they are not viewed as direct competition. Their initiatives are definitely in the population health space, but their scope in terms of PHM programs is unique. As a private, consumer-facing company, they may or may not be based on a specific research concept. For example, a research discovery that benefits patients may have too many hurdles to be deployed in a provider, payer, or population perspective, in which case it makes the most sense to offer the product directly to consumers and patients. These types of things pave the way for network affiliations with academic institutions. Another example is a company that develops a great consumer service or product that ends up unintentionally providing PHM to patients. A nonprofit or government entity may see this and develop a network affiliation to help each other's mission.

From a clinical provider and payer perspective, strategies can be built around care teams. *Care teams* share these roles and responsibilities across organizations, and network affiliations are built. The idea here is that both the providers and payers have PHM initiatives related to things such as closing gaps in care, increasing medication adherence, and decreasing duplication of services. These types of initiatives mean that organizations from both perspectives have staff and systems dedicated to these efforts (Loughran et al., 2017). This also means that it's likely that both perspectives have organizational performance improvement initiatives tied into these efforts.

Alternatively, we have the patient perspective where groups of individuals may create their own communities or networks and seek to build relationships with population perspective entities, such as government agencies or programs dedicated to large-scale PHM initiatives. Perhaps the easiest place for network alliances to form from a population perspective is through *community needs assessments* (CNAs).

Community Needs Assessment

For this discussion, we turn back toward public health as it relates to PHM. CNAs are useful tools in public health and, more recently, population health. They are meant to gather data and assess the community's current state to build a plan for positive and sustainable change. These assessments are used to identify the assets and deficiencies of a community in terms of policy, resources, systems, and the environment. The three outcome categories of a CNA are policy, systems, and environmental change. These three change outcome categories are a great place to start for patient, provider, and payer organizations and groups to build network alliances with population-based organizations that align in both PHM and performance improvement initiatives.

Although there are multiple methods to completing CNAs, we will overview the Centers for Disease Control and Prevention's (CDC) five-step method (CDC, 2013), making sure to pay attention to the parallels with this process and the process for interacting with community public health service providers.

Step 1. Plan for a community needs assessment

1. Assemble a team
2. Build common understanding around
   a. Strategy
   b. Community boundaries
   c. Areas to assess
3. Create questions to ask
4. Develop protocol
5. Examine preexisting data and data to generate

Step 2. Complete the assessment

1. Follow protocol
2. Accumulate data

Step 3. Develop measures

1. Use accumulated data points to develop measures
2. Review new measures as a team

Step 4. Summarize results

1. Analyze data
2. Write summary report of data

Step 5. Create a plan for next steps

1. Articulate assets and deficiencies
2. Rank order findings
3. Identify and reach out to key internal and external stakeholders
4. Work collaboratively to formulate a strategic plan

Since Step 3 puts into action the theory we covered in the beginning of the chapter concerning the development of population health status measures, we begin there to review and connect the theory to its practical application.

Evaluating Community Health Status Measures

To help conceptualize Step 3 of the CDC's five-step method, we return to our previous discussion on population health status measures. Our discussion centered on a couple of frameworks that we will further dissect in this section. Merging the frameworks laid out by Madans and Weeks (2016) (tiers) and Kassler et al. (2017) (more than 2,200 quality measures across 6 domains that double as population health measures) allows for determining specific measures needed to develop population health initiatives. In Madans and Weeks' framework, they lay out three tiers, with the first tier outlining healthy life expectancy (HLE) measures, the second tier deconstructing the HLEs to account for variations across time, and the third tier exploring disease prevalence. While their framework is clinically focused, it's worth exploring how this type of hierarchy could be utilized if you have the data sources to support it. These frameworks give us the ability to visualize measures for capturing outcomes across the scope of population health through specific initiatives. As organizations (both public and private) create policy for their specific initiatives, it is important to align outcome measures to as many other perspective organization collaborators as possible. By doing so, they can develop robust measures.

The formation of new population health measures, Step 3, can and should align with performance improvement goals. Toward this aim, it is important to find existing measures that work well for both PHM and performance initiatives, maintain a focus on measures derived through the Donabedian model (structures, processes, and outcomes), and are used in publicly available data (Donabedian, 2005). To accomplish this, it is best to have people within your organization who are knowledgeable in quality improvement, data analysis, and population health sit down to draft these measures together. After the development of measures, it is a good idea to test their use in small test cases first (Kassler et al., 2015). After the CNA data have been collected and analyzed and a summary report is available, go back to the measures your collaboration team developed and evaluate how they fit into your plan for next steps. Chances are that you will need to reassess these measures a bit since they are more difficult to apply in real life than in theory.

Data Sources

To assist with Step 4 of the CNA, we turn our discussion to data sources. *Data sources* are processes and systems that produce data (a survey or electronic health record). For your initiative(s) to be successful, you should always back PHM and performance improvement with relevant data sources. The proper data sources provide data that allow you to see the past, present, and future of your organization's initiative. Data sources vary drastically; some are ready to use, and others are partially developed. You may even need to develop one from scratch.

The summarization of results, Step 4, can be further understood through the lens of the population perspective of the 4Ps. When thinking about data sources, and how they relate to CNA results, you will need to determine how your improvement initiatives might utilize population perspective data. Health information exchanges (HIEs) are a good data source for organizations that are conducting a CNA, or strategizing about how to create a care coordination program that spans provider and payer organizations. HIEs are designed to allow healthcare organizations and patients share patient medical information. While this is a basic definition, HIEs differ in purpose, scope, and capability. You can start by looking locally and regionally to see what is available in your area. Each HIE may collect different measures, but most HIEs have the objective and data to support PHM initiatives.

Other sources of population perspective include surveillance data and big data. Surveillance data provide tracking information regarding items such as infectious disease, injuries, cancers, and behaviors. Big data refers not only to large volumes of data, but also to data that are extremely complex (Groves et al., 2016). Again, start by looking locally and regionally to see what's available in your area (HealthData.gov is a good practical start). Along these same lines, big data is also available for exploration to find trends and associations related to a whole host of conditions. Depending on the type of CNA you are performing (like those that are environmentally focused), you may want to explore large genetic databases, such as GenBank. Additionally, population perspective data can be collected through community interviews, both by interviewing key community stakeholders and through open-forum committees and town halls. Collecting data in this way allows you to build relationships within the population. There are hundreds of data sources at your disposal; therefore, it is critical to understand what data you may need to ask and answer questions related to your CNA and the PHM initiatives you'd like to pursue as a result of your findings.

After you've chosen your data sources and formulate a plan to collect any new data you may need, you can turn your attention toward integrating disparate data sources (different and not easy to integrate). Since there are few resources focused on integrating data that are stored in different formats, it's something you need to be aware of. For example, let's say you have been granted access to a data set of the medical billing data for your community and it is in the form of databases, your second data set is publicly available in Excel, and your third data set is in the form of PDF files. Even though you planned to use these data sources together, you and your team should develop plans to integrate these data from their different formats so that they can be used toward your PHM and performance improvement initiatives.

While everything we've discussed thus far illustrates great possibility for PHM and performance improvement, it is essential that we remain conscious of data and information to be shared as network alliances are built. A first step in successful long-term networking relationships is to explore and build a common understanding of who generates different data, who owns different data, who has the right to use which data, how data are going to be used, and who has control of changing the answers of these types of questions. This is referred to as *data governance.*

Evaluating Results of Community Needs Assessments

The final step when conducting a CNA is Step 5. The first part of this step includes being able to articulate assets and deficiencies and rank order findings. Creating a plan for next steps also requires that we incorporate the findings from Steps 1–4 into a thorough domain analysis (summary analysis of related items in an area). This deliverable is of value in itself and likely has sections that will hold true for organizations and groups from the patient or consumer, provider, and payer perspectives as well. It is important to note that PHM initiatives are most successful when they combine resources from across perspectives. After taking stock of your assets and rank ordering your findings, you will need to keep in mind which findings would be most useful for addressing and sharing for organizations and groups from multiple perspectives. Moreover, the measures created through this process have the potential to build bridges with other organizations as they create and sustain their own performance improvement initiatives.

Identifying Next Steps and Moving Forward

The final stage of Step 5 includes identifying and communicating with key internal and external stakeholders, and working collaboratively with them to formulate an overall strategic plan. Remember to engage academic institutions in this process to encourage the ability to further the body of knowledge around PHM, to reinforce evidence-based methods, and to leverage a neutral third party (in theory) into the process.

This collaboration will likely produce multiple strategic plans, each focused on what a specific PHM program would address, specific gaps identified, needs in subgroups of the community, and resources available. You will then be able to put into use the process laid out earlier in the chapter regarding how to interact with community public health service providers. The more collaboratively you build these strategic plans, the greater the likelihood of their success.

Population Health Improvement Strategies

Now that we have thoroughly explored the public health population perspective side of PHM, we turn our attention to population health improvement strategies. As we begin this discussion, it's worth taking another look at Figure 9.3 to refresh our memories on what all is involved in the population health improvement cycle. Based on this cycle, how do we practically apply what we have covered thus far to specifically address the following types of PHM initiatives?

■ Special populations
■ Social and cultural determinants of health
■ Wellness programs
■ Chronic disease

How do incentives and economic evaluations play into this process? We will answer these questions using some case studies utilizing the 4Ps.

Special Populations

PHM can be developed to influence the health of special populations. To better illustrate this idea, let's consider the case study below.

CASE STUDY

Imagine your organization is a midsized private payer that works with many providers, several small and midsized, and one large health system. The large health system belongs to a medical academic center, and it has an existing population health initiative. Since the medical center has a population health initiative, your overall goal is to establish a PHM program that begins in the payer organization and aligns with current performance improvement goals strictly focused on a special population of interest.

A first task would be to make partnerships, gather information on available data sources, and then create a PHM program that merges with, and helps, current performance improvement goals. It might take a few months to learn about the providers and health systems you work with. Through this process, relationships with the public health entities in the area can be formed. Another twofold task would be to investigate what senior leadership in the organization understands about population health and become familiar with the processes and programs they currently use to manage their population. Reaching out to researchers at the academic medical center to see if you can find research projects that intentionally or unintentionally focus on population health initiatives would aid the cause. Concurrently, meet with the data analysts, finance director, program leaders, and quality improvement team. These tasks make take from three months to the better part of a year.

Meanwhile, begin exploring data sources (Groves et al., 2016). Because the organization is a payer, it has access to billing (claims) data. In addition, the organization may subscribe to a third-party company that provides analyses on claims data related to medication adherence, chronic diseases, and/or risk stratification for members. Also, explore what, if any, clinical data are provided from electronic health records or lab tests. There may also be a mixture of provider and self-reported social and behavioral data. This self-reported social and behavioral data may include data from wearables and member engagement. Moreover, operational reports are useful to discover data related to cost, quality measures, and performance improvement goals. In combination, these tasks provide access to, and a picture of, the operational and nonoperational data of the organization. In cases such as these, there may be between 10 and 15 disparate sources of data. Figure 9.4 provides a general idea of how these data interact with each other.

Moving forward, it may take three to six months to build a repository for these data. While building, operations might develop new ways to capture data being generated from the payer programs, including wellness education, health coaching, care coordination, and enhanced patient care. The first PHM program the payer initiates might involve a research organization. For example, it might be a communication tool meant to raise awareness related to a special population, such as those with multiple chronic diseases, to facilitate member engagement in payer programs. Figure 9.5 illustrates how such a tool might work.

So, between three months and a year, the PHM program, with its tool, would be ready to go live. How successful would the PHM be? Although it is great in concept and backed by research, it might still fail. Failure could result from a lack of partnership buy-in, both internally and externally. Data

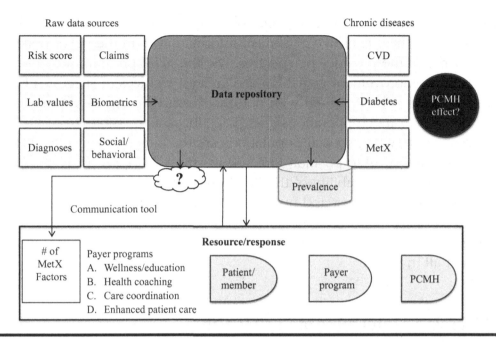

Figure 9.4 Population health data. CVD, cardiovascular disease; MetX, metabolic syndrome.

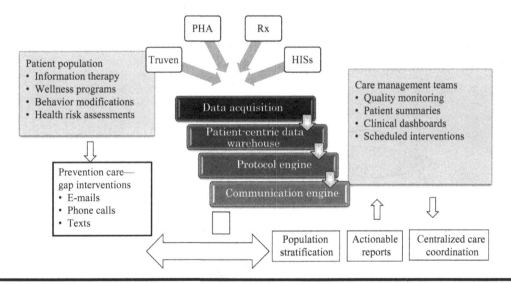

Figure 9.5 Data across integrated network. Biling claims; PHA, population health analytics; HIS, health information systems.

governance issues that were not properly addressed and lack of transparency and vestment from the IT department could affect its success. Lack of engagement from the provider perspective might negatively affect the PHM program. For example, although the communication tool communicates information to members of the special population, participants do not always want to hear sensitive or clinical information from the payer perspective rather than the provider perspective. Did the PHM program incorporate performance improvement goals? For the greatest chances of success, PHM programs need to be designed with not only research partners, if possible, but also as much operations and IT feedback as possible, from the beginning. Also, when special populations are the target audience for PHM programs, it is critical to position PHM efforts from the appropriate perspectives. To ensure sustainability of the PHM program, operations needs to be involved to help align cost and quality measures to performance improvement goals. With as much as the current reporting of quality measures is costing healthcare organizations, working together on these objectives serves to benefit all involved.

Addressing Determinants of Health

Moving on, we pick up where the PHM program example may have fallen short to see what can be improved. This time, the PHM program initiative might start with a layout of where, when, and how the current payer programs overlap with population determinants of health. See Figure 9.6 for what the continuum of care might look like.

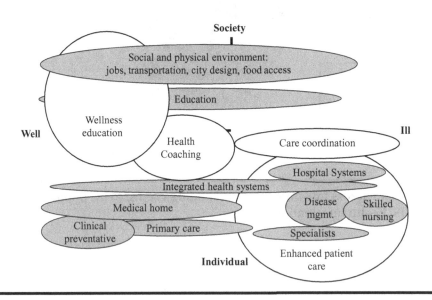

Figure 9.6   Continuum of care.

The possibility of partnering with patient-centered medical homes (PCMHs) to build care teams is an option if better network alliances are established. These care teams could share responsibility for the patients or members and specifically focus on specific determinants of health, such as healthcare for chronic conditions for broader populations. Since this PHM program would be better situated in a clinical environment, measures can be drafted and aligned with the provider organizations that would be helpful for them to meet their performance improvement goals. Since payers are normally better suited for wellness education (rather than providers trying to address wellness in clinical visits to treat issues), the provider organization could give a warm handoff of their patients to the payer for wellness education-based activities. With these additional activities coupled with the previous undertakings, do we think this PHM program would be successful? Focusing on two aspects of population health is the key. Although the number of people who need wellness education is large, many people can be reached at once electronically. And conversely, even though more effort is required to treat patients and members with chronic conditions, developing PHM protocols that span both the provider and payer perspectives helps to eliminate duplication of effort and increase transparency from the patient perspective. Moreover, instead of creating new ways to store data and PHM tools to use, IT can lead the data governance charge, creating more internal buy-in. With all these areas addressed, the focus of the PHM program can turn toward incentives and measures, which we will talk more about in the next section.

Incentives for Health Improvement

As a PHM program such as this matures, there will be an evolution related to patient or member incentives. In the beginning of the PHM program, incentives are normally tied to participation, health outcomes, and penalties. These types of incentives may have limited long-term effects. From the payer perspective, the longer-term success of PHM initiatives can be tied to member payer premium (the amount a person pays per month to have insurance) and medication discounts, and moderate success may be associated with gift cards. Combining efforts with the PCMHs, incentives can be based on praise, such as patient of the month awards. Recognition incentives from the provider perspective may be more powerful that monetary rewards from the payer perspective because of the position providers hold in the mind of participants when compared with payers.

Incentives are necessary for not only members of PHM programs but also those providing the program. An incentive that might work well with provider care teams is data reports supplied by the payer to help care teams be more successful in their organizations. Remember that the payer normally sees a more comprehensive picture of the patient or member continuum of care than the provider does, so payer data may be able to fill in the blanks. This not only serves to increase possible quality measures for provider organizations by bringing in more related data points, but also may bring in cost data. This might make it easier for provider organizations to build more meaningful performance improvement goals based on cost and utilization. The point is that incentives are a continually moving target and will need attention often. Now, what about the larger question of evaluating PHM programs?

Economic Evaluation of Health Programs

PHM seeks to increase utilization of low-cost care, such as preventative care, and decrease utilization of high-cost care, such as hospital admittance (Hodach, 2014). If we want to execute successful PHM programs financially, where do we start? Marino (2017) suggests that we could start by choosing a macromodel. This macromodel allows us to identify the types of low- and high-cost utilization expected to change for each program and track these before and after the PHM initiatives (Marino, 2017). If cost is associated with each service unit, and we break it down per member per month (PMPM), we can subtract the cost of the increased low-cost services from the cost of the decreased high-cost services for a net total savings. From here, we subtract the program costs and get the economic evaluation of the program. To make this the most beneficial, combine types of utilizations across programs for a more accurate picture of your organization's PHM evaluation.

Value-Based Financing and Quality Incentive Programs

To make anything sustainable, there must be incentive to do so. Just like performance improvement, the sustainability of PHM initiatives relies heavily on incentives. How does this work exactly? Well, these incentives are normally based on the reimbursement of provider services. Typically, each single healthcare service is provided and paid for individually, and this is called *fee for service* (FFS). FFS is a reimbursement method where each service performed for a patient is charged. The nature of FFS is to incentivize those providing healthcare to deliver more services. This idea makes sense because the revenue they generate is based on how many individual services they provide. *Value-based financing* (VBF) is an alternative way to pay providers. VBF focuses on the value and quality of services provided. The idea is that the providers would be incentivized to work with patients, other providers, and even payers to improve patient care on specific measures or risk a reduction of pay (Kassler et al., 2015). As elements of the healthcare reform are visited, leaders believe the new VBF model is here to stay (Ollove, 2017). When PHM is tied to pay, there is a higher level of willingness and vestment to link initiatives to performance improvement.

Accountable care organizations (ACOs) are an essential part of the VBF movement. ACOs are made up of collaborating health system providers, such as PCMHs, skilled nursing facilities, and hospitals, who work together to coordinate care and are collectively responsible for the care of their members. ACOs help to offset the risk involved in VBF by working together. In theory, ACOs help eliminate duplication of effort and work toward increasing quality of care (McWilliams et al., 2014). These types of concerted efforts are paramount to the large-scale success of PHM programs.

Quality-based payment mechanisms are enacted through legislation and programs (CMS, 2017). Since these programs are tied to Medicare payments, they are required for other types of payers. The goal is to align legislation and programs with internal quality and performance improvement efforts. This was accomplished through passing the Medicare Access and CHIP Reauthorization Act (MACRA) in 2015. The same year, a value modifier (VM) was put into place for Medicare providers. In simple language, the VM rates providers and rewards them on quality measures by shifting payments from low-performing providers to higher-performing providers. In 2019, the two tracks for the Quality Payment Program (QPP) (the program MACRA authorized) will begin. One is called the Merit-based Incentive Payment System (MIPS), and the other is called Advanced Alternative Payment Models (APMs). MIPS combines previous quality reporting programs into one system with four performance categories (quality, advancing care information, clinical practice improvement activities, and cost), and can affect payments up to 9% positively and negatively (CMS, 2017). APMs are for providers who meet certain requirements by taking patient care even further, and therefore are exempt from MIPS. These providers are eligible for an additional 5% incentive payment. The idea with these initiatives is to align payment and relevant quality measures with the current workflow of providers (Rosenkrantz et al., 2017). The expectation is that if providers go through the effort to meet these challenges for their Medicare patients, they will be willing to implement these methods for all their patients.

With so many opportunities out there, is it becoming easier to align PHM initiatives with these incentives? The answer is yes and no. While these programs offer opportunity, they do not sidestep the need to complete the processes outlined in this chapter. For example, we can look at a case study from Bon Secours Virginia Medical Group (BSVMG) in Richmond, Virginia (Kelly and Rusz, 2017). This group designed a quality-based program that incentivized providers through bonuses rather than a positive or negative affect based on quality. This design was to help providers transition from the FFS model and to prepare them for the coming value-based payment changes. It also allowed them to focus on measures that spanned both PHM and performance improvement. BSVMG was able to increase performance in 10 of its selected measures and maintained performance from the previous year in the remaining three. As next steps, it has expanded its incentive program in scope and provider reach, fine-tuned the thresholds of its measures and created new ones, and moved into more sophisticated reporting on its data.

These new quality and payment structures will also affect industry specialty providers. For example, radiologists are a group that have specialty-specific quality measures (Rosenkrantz et al., 2017). As a result, they have 17 specific measures tailored to their specialty. In addition, they will need to address the ever evolving, and complex, face-to-face patient interaction components to avoid reimbursement penalties. The point is to stay conscious of how VBP may be specifically applied to all aspects of your organization and be prepared to act on multiple levels. There are individual, group or practice, and/or national actions to address these. That brings us to our next section involving building network solutions.

Network Solutions to Health Improvement

Network solutions, including technology and data resources, are a vital part of PHM. Government value-based payment systems provide a common language between organizations within the healthcare delivery system and open the way for building network solutions across organizations. For instance, if we think back to our case study and example focused on PHM for special populations and determinants of health, with VBF now more providers are interested and willing to work together. This is due in large part to the alignment of performance improvement measures across multiple organizations and perspectives. Toward meeting these new quality measures, organizations become more interested in sharing data to receive data that will help them achieve incentives. Increased sharing of these complex data, or big data, means patients can receive the right care, by the right provider, at the right time, for the right value (Groves et al., 2016). The results are more robust versions of PHM initiatives, which in turn have the ability to come full circle with population health, and with positive effects on performance improvement.

The jury is still out on how successful payment incentive programs will be in the long term, and how evolution will morph the programs moving forward. Leveraging the network solutions discovered could play a critical role in the design of new programs, and inform the trajectory of PHM.

Summary

Population health is anchored in public health, but will be advanced by quality management and analytical techniques. There are four main perspectives in the 4Ps framework: patient, provider, payer, and population. This framework can be used to give context to the PHM process. As your organization develops and engages participants in PHM, it is important to remember to parallel these efforts with those related to performance improvement. This can be accomplished through the creation of measures that can be utilized in both efforts identified through CNAs and network alliances. PHM is most sustainable when programs cross organizational perspective with the use of care teams focusing on the wellness and chronic conditions of a population. Nearly all population health improvement strategies rely on value-based incentive models, coupled with evolving technology and data resources.

Key Terms

4Ps, accountable care organization (ACO), care coordination, care teams, community needs assessment, continuum of care, data governance, data sources, determinants of health, fee for service, health disparity, health inequity, healthcare delivery system, network affiliations, population health, PHM, stakeholder, value-based financing

Discussion Questions

1. What is PHM, and how is it different from traditional healthcare?
2. How does an ACO change the way FFS care is delivered?
3. What are the incentives for a hospital or health system to pursue population health improvements?
4. How does PHM support the definition of quality from a value perspective?
5. Should PHM focus on populations with the greatest disparities and health inequity, or areas where the greatest financial opportunities are present? Why?

References

CDC (Centers for Disease Control and Prevention) (2013). Community needs assessment. Available at www.cdc.gov.

Chan A, Saito Y, and Robine JM (2016). International perspectives on summary measures of population health in an aging world. *Journal of Aging Health*, 28(7), 1119–1123.

CMS (Centers for Medicare and Medicaid Services) (2017). MACRA. Available at https://www.cms.gov/Medicare/Quality-Initiatives-Patient-Assessment-Instruments/Value-Based-Programs/MACRA-MIPS-and-APMs/MACRA-MIPS-and-APMs.html.

Donabedian A (2005). Evaluating the quality of medical care. *The Milbank Quarterly*, 83(4), 691–729.

Groves P, Kayyali B, Knott D, and Kuiken SV (2016). The 'big data' revolution in healthcare: Accelerating value and innovation. *McKinsey Quarterly*. Available at www.pharmatalents.es/assets/files/Big_Data_Revolution.pdf.

Hodach R (2014). *Provider-Led Population Health Management: Key Strategies for Healthcare in the Next Transformation*. Bloomington, IN: AuthorHouse.

Kassler WJ, Howerton M, Thompson A, Cope E, Alley DE, and Sanghavi D (2017). Population health measurement at Centers for Medicare & Medicaid Services: Bridging the gap between public health and clinical quality. *Journal of Population Health Management*, 20(3), 173–180.

Kassler WJ, Tomoyasu N, and Conway PH (2015). Beyond a traditional payer—CMS's role in improving population health. *New England Journal of Medicine*, 372(2), 109–111.

Kelly DL and Rusz S (2017). Value-based compensations for primary care, a success story. *Healthcare Financial Management*, March.

Kindig D and Stoddart G (2003). What is population health? *American Journal of Public Health*, 93(3), 380–383.

Kindig D (2015). What are we talking about when we talk about population health? Health Affairs Blog, April 6, 2015. DOI:10.1377/hblog20150406.046151.

Loughran J, Puthawala T, Sutton BS, Brown LE, Pronovost PJ, and DeFilippis AP (2017). The cardiovascular intensive care unit—An evolving model for health care delivery. *Journal of Intensive Care Medicine*, 32(2), 116–123.

Madans JH and Weeks JD (2016). A framework for monitoring progress using summary measures of health. *Journal of Aging and Health*, 28(7), 1299–1314.

Marino D (2017). Building a value model for population health management. *Healthcare Financial Management*, March.

McWilliams JM, Landon BE, Chernew ME, and Zaslavsky AM (2014). Changes in patients' experiences in Medicare accountable care organizations. *New England Journal of Medicine*, 371(18), 1715–1724.

Ollove M (2017). How this Vermont experiment improves patient health at lower cost. PBS Newshour. Available at http://www.pbs.org/newshour/rundown/vermont-experiment-improves-patient-health-lower-cost/.

Reidy J, Halvorson J, Makowski S, Katz D, Weinstein B, McCluske C, and Tjia J (2017). Health system advance care planning culture change for high-risk patients: The promise and challenges of engaging providers, patients, and families in systematic advance care planning. *Journal of Palliative Medicine*, 20(4), 388–394.

Rosenkrantz AB, Nicola GN, Allen B, Hughes DR, and Hirsch JA (2017). MACRA, MIPS, and the new Medicare Quality Payment Program: An update for radiologists. *Journal of the American College of Radiology*, 14(3), 316–323.

Schroeder SA (2007). We can do better—improving the health of the American people. *New England Journal of Medicine*, 357(12), 1221–1228.

Chapter 10

Future of Quality Improvement

Tiffany Champagne-Langabeer and Rigoberto Delgado

Contents

> Productivity is being able to do things that you were never able to do before.
>
> **Franz Kafka**
> *Author*

Introduction

As described throughout this book, there are a number of different factors impacting the performance of healthcare organizations. These trends require changes in how analysts approach projects and how organizations deliver quality management. Population health management is one of the biggest opportunities, as it encourages health systems to focus on achieving better value, outcomes, cost position, and quality. In this chapter, we discuss significant trends and the future of quality management. We provide recommendations for performance improvement professionals in the healthcare industry.

Trends

Despite the political context surrounding healthcare reimbursement, financial and operational metrics have improved over the past few years compared with in prior decades. Return on assets (ROA) for all hospitals and health systems reviewed by one of the largest credit rating agencies was reported at 4.8% for 2015, well above that of most other industries (Moody's Investor Service, 2016). Other performance outcomes still have significant work to do to improve population health outcomes and strategic indicators of health system success.

Figure 10.1 summarizes the key trends impacting quality management in the coming years for hospitals and health systems. We will discuss each of these below.

One of the primary trends we are seeing in healthcare involves the significantly greater use of collaboration, both internally and externally. Partnerships, network affiliations, and coordinated care across accountable care organizations all point to greater levels of collaboration.

These interorganizational partnerships can take many forms, such as community projects involving public health departments, emergency medical services (EMS) agencies, or other providers in systems of care, and are becoming much more common. Performance improvement projects that once tended to focus only within an organization will be stretched to explore how different organizations can work together toward a common goal. One way of doing this is through the sharing of interorganizational data. The pervasiveness of health information exchanges (HIEs) will continue. Use of HIE data to improve care for patients should be encouraged and expanded. This is an area that is rapidly evolving and will ultimately serve patients as they transition from providers or levels of care within a community.

We will also see even greater levels of partnership between payers and providers, and the community and health systems. In an

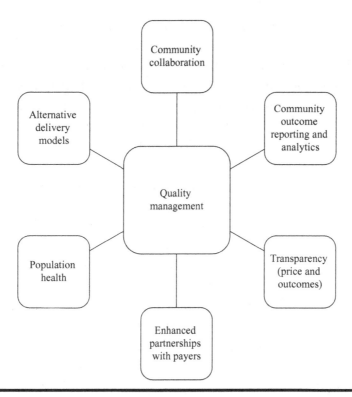

Figure 10.1   Trends impacting quality management.

atmosphere of value-based care, a close working relationship between the insurance companies who pay the bills and the clinicians who provide the services is essential. Payers have an advantage in this respect and have a longer time frame of experience in value-based care. They have insight into longitudinal claims data for patients and have been stratifying risk profiles as a business model for years. *Population health management* will emerge as a discipline that integrates these data from payers and uses them to target interventions focused on improving patients' health status and cost reductions. When payers focus on the outcomes that encourage a healthier population and create financial incentives to maintain patient health, the community prospers. To some extent, a focus on value and outcomes will encourage fewer "silos" and more teamwork between payers and providers. We will talk more about this in the next section.

To make these interorganizational challenges, leadership will have to focus on all outcomes, not just financial ones. Although financial performance, such as reducing costs or improving revenues, will continue to be a key challenge, more outcomes will be shared between partners and become a source of value. Leadership of quality and organizations will need to have a much more strategic perspective on healthcare.

The need for transparency will also continue. *Transparency* is an attribute of being clear, so that things can be seen distinctly. Transparency of services (e.g., clearly stated pricing, performance outcomes, and volume of care provided) will become a goal for many organizations, as this will be required by payers to continue in networks. Competition based on the transparency of price and outcomes should become the norm. Patients will engage more fully as they demand transparency in the cost of healthcare services as they compare prices between providers. Healthcare leaders who can present this information in an accessible form to the community will have a competitive advantage. Making an organization's performance data visible and transparent will become a role for quality and performance improvement management.

There will also be an increased interest in alternative delivery models for healthcare. An *alternative delivery model* is an approach that is different from traditional care, and utilizes diverse information, facilities, processes, and systems to provide care to patients. Alternative delivery models seek to reduce costs and improve outcomes through nontraditional means. The *patient-centered medical home* (PCMH) is an arrangement that provides patients with a centralized physician to coordinate care across the spectrum, with the goal of reducing the need for specialists and other escalations of care (e.g., emergency services). PCMHs are often known for their preventive services, such as annual exams and vaccinations. Another example of an alternative model is the use of a retail urgent care clinic. These same-day drop-in clinics provide an appealing model for patients who may need to see a clinician on a weekend or otherwise would not wait in an emergency room for a primary care–related need.

Telehealth is a specific alternative delivery model that involves information technology. *Telehealth* is the use of audio and visual technology to deliver care and other services. As recent legislation continues to encourage usage of telehealth, it will become far more routine than it is today, and will be offered in more than a small number of service lines. Currently, telehealth is widely used for specialties such as dermatology and psychology, and is near ubiquitous in radiology and for the care of veterans and offshore workers. Strides are being made to extend specialists to rural areas for vascular neurology consultations for lifesaving stroke care using telehealth as well.

Other technologies, such as remote monitoring, will allow providers to care for patients without entering the physical walls of an organization. Like telehealth, remote monitoring allows patients who are distant from their provider to send follow-up data, such as daily weight, blood pressure, and other heart measurements, at regular intervals, often delaying the need for in-office follow-up care. This technology can be used in other ways; for example, some have suggested that the more widespread use of wearable devices on our wrists can provide common data that allow a patient to control his or her own healthcare. Some have called this "democratizing medicine" (Topol, 2015). Patient-generated data will need to be integrated into healthcare systems and processes, and this will be a key topic for years to come. The challenge for quality managers will be how to incorporate these new data into performance improvement programs as alternatives and process changes for services that need fixed.

Incorporating data from multiple sources, including those from claims and alternate delivery methods, will continue to be a challenge and an opportunity for those with the skill sets to produce and analyze robust databases. Community outcomes reporting will focus attention on regional leaders in heart disease, orthopedic medicine, emergency care, and other specialties as hospitals publish their analytical dashboards, comparing their services to those of other hospitals in their region. Patients will have choices in where they go for their care, and they will have greater access and ownership of their healthcare data. In response, healthcare leaders will share accountability across the spectrum with providers, payers, and the patients they serve for the health of their communities.

Population Health Analytics

As discussed in Chapter 9, population health relates to the maintenance or improvement of a specific population group, members of a hospital plan, or an accountable care organization (Health Research and Educational Trust, 2012). Recently, however, researchers have suggested extending the focus to a broader level that encompasses not only panel segments of the population (or hospital level), but also entire communities located within given geographical boundaries, or target segments defined by age or demographic characteristics (Hacker and Walker, 2012). This view implies significant changes to the traditional scope of healthcare provision, and it becomes relevant as healthcare providers are increasingly reimbursed based on sick-ness prevention (value-based medicine), rather than disease treatment.

Successful implementation of population health strategies depends on understanding physical and socioeconomic factors influencing the health of a community's determinants (Keyes and Galea, 2016). It relies on multi-institutional collaborations involving hospitals, federally qualified health centers, and public health organizations, as well as multisectorial col-laborations involving education, private industry, and others (Kindig and Isham, 2014).

Recent healthcare legislation encourages reaching the higher levels of population aggregation by means of horizontal multisectorial cooperation. Clearly, this level implies harnessing the capabilities of diverse community resources in search of a true community-based population health strategy. How to establish working population health networks is an ongoing strategic challenge.

The development of big data management systems and the introduc-tion of interoperability software, which allows data exchange between data repositories, have resulted in opportunities to apply high-end analytical tools. These changes, coupled with value-based health policies, have cre-ated a demand for professionals with expertise in data analytics and strat-egy planning. Therefore, the role of business analysts has transitioned from data consolidation and reporting to data management and application in the design, deployment, and evaluation of population health strategies at the enterprise level. However, analysts involved in population health have roles that extend beyond defining risk profiles for hospital patient populations, and can involve the use of analytics at the community and regional levels for defining appropriate healthcare policies. It is at these levels that the applica-tion of complex analytical approaches makes sense, particularly to evaluate the effect of multi-institutional collaborative initiatives.

This is illustrated in the model of population health domains. The vertical axis represents the unit of analysis, beginning with the individual provider. The horizontal axis shows the degree of institutional integra-tion, or cooperation required to achieve each level of population aggre-gation. The basic level is coordination of clinical departments found in a single provider, such as a hospital. The next level is vertical coordination of institutions within the healthcare sector. A higher degree of coordina-tion is achieved when institutions from several distinct sectors (e.g., pub-lic safety, healthcare providers, and private sector organizations) engage in closely complementary actions aimed at improving the health of the population or providing services that indirectly result in better health (e.g., higher education programs).

Figure 10.2 illustrates the change in data usage as institutions evolve from a single-provider focus to that of participating components in a coordinated horizontal population health group.

At the single-provider level, the function of a data analyst entails mostly data consolidation for reporting on overall performance. This function can be defined as based on business intelligence systems with interoperability between functional areas (e.g., clinical records and finance) and limited interoperability with data systems outside the enterprise. At this level, it is possible that the hospital organization might be conducting predictive analytics to identify patient groups with similar risk profiles and with the purpose of controlling costs. The goal of the analytics function involves mostly managerial economics, such as cost analysis and forecasting.

With the involvement of many provider institutions in the vertical coordination space (preventive, primary, secondary, and tertiary care institutions), the complexity level of analytical tools increases, as well as the capacity and willingness to share data across institutions within the healthcare sector. The improvement of connectivity across healthcare organizations is a national priority for improving decision making, eliminating redundant procedures, reducing cost, and providing better care, which favors the establishment of multiprovider coordination (Office of the National Coordinator for Health IT,

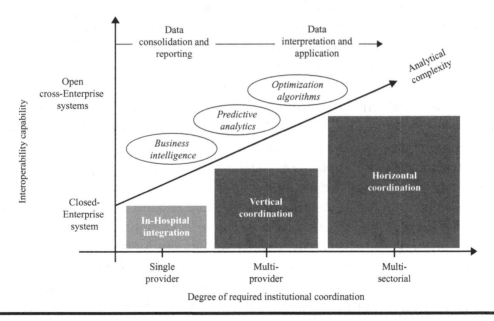

Figure 10.2   Continuum of population health analytical complexity.

2012). Analysts at this level are likely to participate less in data consolidation and more in data interpretation. Establishing a functional analytics infrastructure is a requirement at this level to allow data consolidation and the use of complex tools, such as logistic regression, data mining (supervised and unsupervised), neural networks, and fuzzy logic (Popovic, 2016).

Population health analytics is the use of analytics to support population health management. The primary goal is to identify segments of patient populations and needs with a view to coordinate functions across different health organizations. Multidisciplinary (e.g., statistics and policy analysis) participation becomes important at this level. One recent example involves a study on the optimization of mobile clinics providing vaccination services to underserved school-aged children (Delgado and Roy, 2017). This study brought together experts in health economics, epidemiology, medical services, geographical information systems (GISs), and traffic engineering, and representatives from eight different healthcare and educational institutions. The analytical approaches included GIS population analysis, cost of disease projections, data mining, and optimization modeling. The results showed improvements of up to 50% in the number of vaccines provided using the same resources invested prior to the study. The overall focus of these population health analyses is the cost of care reduction through disease prevention. However, an alternate function of population health analytics is the ability to predict future sources of disease to implement preventive interventions. An example is the application of GIS population data combined with historical demographic data to create epidemic risk profiles for defined segments of populations. Thus, the focus of multi-institutional vaccination campaigns would be directed at target populations showing the highest risk of infection proliferation (Roy and Delgado, 2017).

The multisectorial level, which implies the close coordination of institutions across a horizontal spectrum of sectors (e.g., healthcare, education, and public safety), requires the highest degree of analytical power and the greatest interoperability capability. The role of analytics at this point is strictly data interpretation and application to strategic resource deployment; data consolidation is done at the institution-specific level first, and combined automatically at the multi-institutional level, as a second step, through cross-enterprise interoperability. As shown in Figure 2.2, analytical complexity is extreme given the need to analyze multiple community health factors and institutional resource constraints. There are no existing examples of organizations working at the level of horizontal coordination as defined here, and there is a significant opportunity to define the type of analytics that can be used. Given the expected participation of various intersectorial organizations, the use of input/output economic models seems appropriate. These are models that combine the resource constraints of providers and service demand needs in a community to obtain optimal distribution of resources at the local or regional level. The application of similar methods shows promise in defining service priorities and obtaining regional development plans. Another issue of importance in the horizontal coordination space is the proper functioning of multisectorial organizations. It is not clear if population health analytics can play a role, but it is important to use objective analysis to define incentives for creating sustainable collaborations. For example, it is possible to formulate economic models of competition so that healthcare institutions can work with other competing and cooperating organizations.

There are a significant number of issues to be resolved related to healthcare legislation that impact healthcare financing and provider reimbursements. However, it is likely that pressures for controlling increasing costs in healthcare will result in a higher interest in preventive care and value-based medicine. Under such a scenario, population health analytics will remain a clear source of competitive advantage for healthcare providers, and the need for expertise in population health analytics and use of data-rich analytical tools will continue to increase. Further, the consolidations in the healthcare industry, including the emergence of megaspecialist groups and multistate health systems, will result in significant economies of scale, enhanced consolidation of patient data, and better opportunities to apply data analysis in population health.

Recommendations for Quality and Performance Professionals

Based on these evolving trends, there are five summary recommendations for quality and performance improvement professionals.

1. Get comfortable with big data. Seek to understand what data sources are available, including within your own organization and outside. This could be data from claims, market scans, other providers, HIEs, and insurance payers. Knowing how data are structured and how to integrate them for better decision making will help quality and performance improvement analysts add more value to their organizations.
2. Develop new analytical skills. Even though all these data are available, they must be accessible and usable. Some organizations have access to

really good information technology analysts to help with database and reporting, but others do not. Try to learn the basics of interfaces and extraction, so you can obtain data when you need them. Then, learn a good analytical software and make sure you know all the basics from this book. Examining descriptive statistics, trends, patterns, and visualizations is essential to using data for performance improvement. Software skills are equally important, so try to understand how to use the basic statistical packages (e.g., SPSS, SAS, R, and Statgraphics), visualization (e.g., Tableau and ArcGis), and process management (e.g., Simul8 and Visio).

3. Continuous learning should be the norm. Learning organizations require all of us to constantly be on the top of our game. Learn about new and evolving techniques and analyses. Take courses in project management. Keep working on developing better interpersonal skills for teamwork and collaboration. Learn budgeting and accounting, and how your organization reports its financials. Try to learn one new thing every week, and by the end of each year you will have amassed a library of new knowledge.

4. Develop your leadership skills. Leading project teams is a start. Taking classes in a business school or healthcare program is another way to learn theory. More importantly, practice what you have learned. Leadership involves putting other people first and developing others' potential by using facilitation and interpersonal skills to keep people engaged and participating. Learning to identify what motivates others and encouraging teamwork are critical skills. Leadership will help analysts and project managers continue to move up the organizational hierarchy.

5. Get recognized through certification, licenses, and fellowships. Continuing education is vital, and along the way a certification, license, or fellowship might also be necessary. It might be useful to consider getting a Project Management Professional (PMP) certification or a certification in data analytics, or becoming a fellow of an organization such as Healthcare Information and Management Systems Society (HIMSS). Whatever you decide, learn new things. Certifications and other recognition provide evidence of this to yourself and your organizations.

Summary

There are challenges ahead for quality professionals in the coming years. It is likely that pressures for controlling increasing costs in healthcare will result in a higher interest in preventive care and value-based medicine.

Under such a scenario, performance improvement competencies will remain a clear source of competitive advantage for healthcare providers. Understanding changes in population health management will be valuable for performance improvement professionals, as value-based care focuses health systems on quality, costs, and outcomes. Quality management and performance improvement will become more cross-functional and interorganizational in years to come. Preparing for this future will require expertise in quality management, analytics, and population health. Be responsible for your own career by learning, leading, and loving your job.

Key Terms

Alternative delivery model, patient-centered medical home, population health analytics, population health management, telehealth, transparency

Discussion Questions

1. What opportunities will data sharing between organizations provide health systems?
2. How can patient-generated data (e.g., from a wearable device) help to improve care delivery?
3. How should performance improvement analysts better integrate HIEs and interorganizational partnerships in their project portfolio?
4. What is population health analytics' greatest potential?

References

Delgado R and Roy D (2017). Cost-effectiveness of partial vaccinations: A proposed methodology. Presentation at the 12th World Congress in Health Economics, International Health Economics Association, July 10, 2017, Boston, MA.

Hacker K and Walker DK (2012). Achieving population health in accountable care organizations. *American Journal of Public Health*, 103(7), 1163–1167.

Health Research and Educational Trust (2012). Managing population health: The role of the hospital. Available at www.hpoe.org.

Keyes KM and Galea S (2016). Setting the agenda for a new discipline: Population health science. *American Journal of Public Health*, 106(4), 633–634.

Kindig DA and Isham G (2014). Population health improvement: A community health business model that engages partners in all sectors. *Frontiers in Health Services Management*, 30(4), 3–20.

Moody's Investor Service (2016). U.S. not-for-profit hospital 2015 medians report, September. Available at www.moodys.com/research/Moodys-Preliminary-FY-2015-US-NFP-hospital-medians-indicate-continuing--PR_347650.

Office of the National Coordinator for Health IT, US Department of Health and Human Services (2012). Connecting health and care for the nation: A 10-year vision to achieve an interoperable health IT infrastructure. Available at www.healthit.gov.

Popovic JR (2016). Distributed data networks: A blueprint for big data sharing and healthcare analytics. *Annals of the New York Academy of Science*, 1387(1), 105–111.

Roy R and Delgado R (2017). Measuring economic outcome of preventive health services: A proposed new approach. Presentation at the 12th World Congress in Health Economics, International Health Economics Association, July 10, 2017, Boston, MA.

Topol E (2015). *The Patient Will See You Now*. New York: Basic Books.

Glossary of Key Terms

4Ps: Patient, provider, payer, and population perspectives in population health.

5S: A technique in Lean that helps to create a working environment for optimizing value-added activities. Sort, set in order, shine, standardize, and sustain.

Accountable care organization: An organization comprised of collaborating health system providers (such as patient-centered medical homes, skilled nursing facilities, and hospitals) that work together to coordinate care and are collectively responsible for the care of their members.

Activity: A task that occurs at a specific point in time, has a duration that is random, and shows a known probability distribution. Used in process modeling.

Administrative data: Data gathered by a healthcare organization that are used for administrative purposes, such as billing or regulatory reporting.

Algorithm: A formula or calculation used to solve problems in a model.

Alternative delivery model: An approach that is different from traditional care, and utilizes diverse information, facilities, processes, and systems to provide care to patients. Alternative delivery models seek to reduce costs and improve outcomes through nontraditional means.

Analytics: The study of operational data to identify trends or relationships that can advise management decision making.

Arrival event: A term used in queuing theory to describe when an entity arrives to the system.

As-is process: Process map that depicts the actual, current process in place prior to any process engineering.

Average length of stay (ALOS): The average number of days a patient stays in a facility, measured from admission to discharge. An inpatient metric, which is calculated as the number of patient days during a period divided by the number of discharges.

Balanced scorecard: A graphical display of the set of measures that gives top managers a fast and comprehensive view of their organization. A type of performance scorecard.

Benchmarking: Comparison of a key performance measurement relative to that of the competition or other leading organizations. The process of seeking best practices among better-performing organizations, with intentions of applying those internally.

Benefit: Those gains in performance accrued to a process as a result of focused effort from a well-coordinated project. Perceived value that will be achieved with new service or technology.

Benefit realization: The process and guidelines for measuring and ensuring that a project or program delivers expected performance benefits (e.g., stated goals).

Big data: Extremely large data sets that can be analyzed to reveal trends and patterns.

Bottleneck: A choke point, or a point in a process where capacity is limited and effectively reduces the number of outputs due to physical or logical constraints.

Brainstorming: A team approach to generating ideas and solving problems.

Business concept: A document that clarifies the design or plan for something new, such as an organization or new service line.

Capacity: The organization's ability to deliver something. The amount of resources or assets that exist to serve the demand.

Care coordination: Management of care activities between and across industry services (providers and facilities) for individuals and groups.

Care team: Shared roles and responsibilities across organizations and network affiliations.

Cause-and-effect analysis: A technique to identify the feasible causes that are related to a specific problem. Often results in a diagram, called cause-and-effect diagram or fishbone diagram.

Change: Transition from one state to another state, or a process of becoming different.

Change management: Structured attempt to identify and manage alterations to a plan across projects and organizations.

Clinical data: Data gathered by a healthcare organization that document the findings of patient examination, treatments or services provided, and outcomes of care to the patient.

Coefficient of variation: A measure of variability, defined as the standard deviation divided by the mean.

Collaboration: The act of working together to achieve a common purpose. Similar to teamwork, involving partnerships.

Community needs assessment: A population health tool to gather data, assess the community's current state of affairs, and plan for positive and sustainable change.

Competitiveness: The ability of an organization to provide goods and services that are superior to those of its rivals, and produce value for customers and long-term sustainability.

Confidence interval: A term used in statistics and in simulation modeling. Provides a confidence estimate (i.e., $100 - \alpha\%$) of where the mean of a process falls within the interval.

Constraint: Place where process throughput is limited. Also known as a bottleneck.

Continuum of care: Range of patient's healthcare provided over a period of time.

Cost of quality: The sum of all costs associated with providing inferior, error-prone, or poor-quality services.

Critical path method (CPM): A project management technique used to estimate the most desirable path of key activities necessary to complete the project on time.

Culture: Core values and beliefs shared by all employees and management in an organization.

Current Procedural Terminology (CPT): A code set used to describe procedures and services provided to a patient in a healthcare setting.

Current state: A representation of a process as it currently exists, prior to any changes.

Dashboard: Visual summary of the key performance indicators' status toward goals. Sometimes referred to as a performance scorecard or balanced scorecard, depending on the types of metrics it contains.

Database: A structured set of data elements stored in a computer, made up of tables.

Data cleansing: The process of validating and fixing incomplete, inaccurately coded, or corrupt data.

Data-driven management: The use of data to drive decisions through proven and established management practices.

Data governance: The process of understanding and controlling how data are used.

Data sources: Processes and systems that produce data.

De-bottleneck: To eliminate constraints or obstacles that limit capacity or throughput.

Decision: A choice between two or more alternatives.

Decision analysis: A process of separating or decomposing a complex decision, incorporating uncertainty and dynamic assumptions into algorithms to generate alternative choices. The use of analytic methods to make better decisions.

Defect: An instance where a process fails to meet the customer's requirement.

Defect per million opportunities: Measure of the relative proportion of defects in a process. A Six Sigma term defined as the number of defects in a process divided by the total number of opportunities for defects, multiplied by 10^6. DPMO is used to convert to a Six Sigma level (1, 2, 3, etc.) where 3.4 DPMO is 6 sigma and 691,500 DPMO is 1 sigma.

Determinants of health: Factors that influence population health status, including genetics, behaviors, healthcare, and social and physical environments.

Discovery: A thorough investigation of the present environment and collection of evidence.

Discrete-event simulation: Dynamic modeling of discrete (separate) events to predict overall process and system behaviors.

DMAIC: Define, measure, analyze, improve, control. The methodology behind Six Sigma.

Donabedian model: Structured framework for examining quality of care: Based on inputs, process, and outcomes:

Electronic data interchange: A process that allows organizations to share key pieces of data through standardized electronic means.

Electronic health record (EHR): A comprehensive longitudinal electronic record that stores patient health data in a hospital or clinic, including patient demographics, prior medical history, interventions performed, laboratory and test results, and medications. Often a collection of clinical health applications.

Electronic medical record: A computer application used in healthcare organizations to document examination findings, procedures and services provided to patients, results of diagnostic tests, and plans of care.

Event: The culmination of an activity, which can change the state of a process. Used in process modeling.

Evidence: Empirical data, or proof, supporting a decision or position.

Evidence-based management: The use of proven and established organizational practices to improve decisions and results.

Failure modes and effects analysis (FMEA): Tool for documenting potential failures in a process, causes, risks, and potential solutions.

Fee for service: A reimbursement method where each service performed for a patient is charged, to incentivize those providing healthcare to deliver more services. This is the opposite of value-based financing or bundled payments.

Fishbone: A diagram that visually represents root cause analysis, which makes it easier for teams to conceptualize and take action. Cause-and-effect diagram. Also known as an Ishikawa diagram.

Five whys: A Lean technique of asking the question why multiple times to understand the root cause of an issue.

Flowchart: A visual diagram depicting the sequential actions, steps, inputs, and decisions in a process.

Future state: A representation of the desired end state of a process, which should have higher value and is more streamlined:

Gantt chart: Used as a project plan in large projects to show progress, resources, constraints, and timelines.

Gap: The difference between the current and future states.

Gap analysis: Documentation of the differences between the current state of a process and the desired future state. Focused on gaps in people, process, and technology.

Goals: Broad, long-term statements of an ideal future state. The amount of improvement the organization is trying to achieve.

Healthcare delivery system: Interaction of organizations working together to provide healthcare services to a population.

Healthcare Effectiveness Data and Information Set (HEDIS): A detailed database of quality measures used to assess physician quality, used by health plans and insurance providers.

Health disparity: Differences between outcomes or care in populations.

Health inequity: An avoidable or preventable health outcome.

Health information exchange: A technology infrastructure that enables secure digital exchange of standardized information across organizations involved in the care of a patient.

ICD-10: International Classification of Diseases, Tenth Edition. A code set that describes diseases or injuries or inpatient surgical procedures.

Improve: To make something better. Positive change.

Institutional provider: A healthcare provider entity, such as a hospital, skilled nursing facility, or hospice.

Interorganizational collaboration: Partnerships between different organizations designed to improve the competitive advantage for the respective parties or organizations involved:

Kaizen: Japanese word for continuous improvement, usually achieved in small increments.

Kanban: Visual card process that provides process flow and helps identify bottlenecks: Used in Lean methodologies:

Key: With reference to a normalized database, key is a variable that is common among tables in a database that can be used to join rows from different tables together.

Key performance indicator: Quantitative measure of performance used to evaluate the success that an organization has in meeting established objectives. A limited number of performance metrics that quantify operating results in critical areas, typically focused around profitability, debt management, efficiency, capital, and strategic categories.

Kurtosis: Data observations that are heavily tailed in one direction or another.

Lean: A methodology for quality improvement focused on removing waste and unnecessary steps from a process. Improvements tend to focus on increased speed, improved flexibility, reduced lot sizes, increased customization, and reduced waste.

Learning organization: Organization that improves actions and behaviors through new information that is regularly created and shared:

Low-hanging fruit: Benefits that will be easily captured by focusing on those process steps that are the least costly and complex to rapidly improve.

Management engineering: The application of engineering principles to healthcare processes. A discipline focused on designing optimal management and information systems and processes, using tools from engineering, mathematics, and social sciences. Application of engineering principles to healthcare processes.

Management systems: The framework of all processes, policies, procedures, standards, and other documentation that defines how an organization should behave in order to achieve its purpose.

Master patient index: A table in a healthcare organization database that lists patient demographic information that is used by computer applications in the organization.

Mean: The mathematical average of all values in a series of observations.

Median: The middle value in a range of observations.

Metric: Measurement that includes a distinct numerator and denominator developed specifically to measure the established goal or objective. Also known as a key performance indicator (KPI).

Mission accountability: Holding nonprofit organizations accountable for directly achieving their mission. A component of organizational performance in healthcare that aligns community and organization goals.

Modifier: An adjunct to a Common Procedural Terminology (CPT) code that provides further description of the service or procedure.

Morbidity: A measure of the rate of illness.

Mortality: A measure of the rate of incidence for deaths.

National Drug Code (NDC): A code set that describes medications by manufacturer, medication name, and packaging.

Net present value (NPV): A method for converting future cash inflows (benefits) and outflows (expenditures) into a single value in today's terms. Used to evaluate whether a project makes financial sense.

Network affiliations: Organizations that work together to build affiliations and relationships.

Normal distribution: Representation of data, where a larger, denser concentration of observations is toward the center, and less on the tails. Also known as a bell curve.

Normalized database: A database that has been organized into multiple tables to minimize the duplication of values and uses a key to relate rows from different tables to each other.

Objectives: Specific, short-term, quantifiable statements that are readily measurable.

On time, on budget, on scope: Key outcome metrics for the success of a project. On time refers to delivering a project within the timeline set at the initial project planning phase. On budget refers to keeping costs under budget. On scope refers to not exceeding (or minimizing) the intended objectives of the project as defined.

Operational excellence: A term used to describe an organization that continuously seeks to improve its productivity, business processes, and overall effectiveness.

Outcomes: Results of an activity or event, which is commonly expressed as a metric to gauge the success or failure of a process model.

Patient-centered medical home: An arrangement that provides patients with a centralized physician to coordinate care across the spectrum, with the goal of reducing the need for specialist and other escalations of care:

PDCA: Plan–do–check–act. A methodology for continuous improvement. Sometimes referred to as plan–do–study–act.

Performance: The inputs, process, and results for specific areas. Represents the attainment of key goals, strategic advantage, or other outcomes desirable to an organization. Measured by outcomes, such as financial margins, quality, and patient satisfaction.

Performance improvement: An approach that analyzes, measures, and changes business and clinical processes to improve outcomes or results.

Performance management: Process by which organizations align their resources, systems, and employees to strategies and objectives.

Performance scorecard: Visual summary of the key performance indicators' status toward goals. Sometimes referred to as a balanced scorecard, depending on the types of metrics it contains. Also known as a dashboard.

Population health: Distribution of health outcomes for a group of individuals.

Population health analytics: Use of analytics to support population health management, with a goal to identify segments of patient populations and needs with a view to coordinate functions across different health organizations.

Population health management (PHM): Management of a population's health outcomes and costs, through interventions utilizing aggregation of clinical, operational, behavioral, and billing data.

Portfolio management: The systematic governance of projects with an aim toward maximizing value or utility across the organization, while managing risks.

Predictive modeling: The use of an algorithm and software on large data sets to forecast potential outcomes.

Process: Set of linked activities and tasks that are performed in sequence to achieve a specific goal or produce a deliverable.

Process capability index: A measure for gauging the extent to which a process meets the customer's expectations (typically expressed as C_p or C_{pk}).

Process engineering: The careful scrutiny of a current state process to identify value creation opportunities, such as eliminating handoffs or steps in the process.

Process flowchart: Diagram depicting the flows or activities in a process.

Process mapping: Visual flowchart of ordered activities in a discrete process. Also known as flowchart.

Process redesign: Process improvement. Redesigning a process to streamline, simplify, and enhance value.

Productivity: The ratio of outputs to inputs for a specific process or system.

Professional provider: A healthcare provider, such as a physician or group of physicians.

Program evaluation and review technique (PERT): A project management technique to estimate the time it will take to complete a project. PERT = [Optimistic time (O) + Pessimistic time (P) + 4× Most likely time (4M)]/6.

Project: An organized effort involving a sequence of activities that are temporarily being performed to achieve a desired outcome.

Project charter: A document that describes the project's purpose, plans, assumptions, and roles.

Project management: The application of knowledge, skills, tools, and techniques to a project in order to achieve project success.

Project management office: A group of professionals that assist management in developing structure and standards for more sophisticated management of projects, especially those in information technology.

Project manager: The individual who leads the planning and daily activities to achieve the project deliverables.

Project strategic alignment: An approach to measuring the degree of similarity between a project and the organization's strategic priorities.

Prototype: Rapid development of a working model that resembles the future state. Emphasizes rapid application design approach, in which users and developers work collaboratively together to shorten development lead times.

Quality: Perception of the level of value a customer places on an organization's outputs, and the degree to which they meet established specifications and benchmarks.

Quality management: A management philosophy focused on systematically improving processes and performance.

Query: A search process that gathers data based on specified conditions.

Range: The difference between high and low values in a range of observations.

Relative value unit: Weighted volume unit, typically used in ancillary and other departments where traditional volume counts vary dramatically in terms of length, complexity, or intensity of service provided.

Resources: Inputs (e.g., raw materials and personnel) used in a process.

Return on investment (ROI): A measure of the total project return, expressed in discounted dollar values over time, which expresses the relationship between benefits and costs.

Revenue code: A unique code used by institutional providers to define the department in which a service was provided to a patient.

Risk: Uncertainty of events or outcomes that could negatively impact outcomes. Possibility of suffering harm or loss, as during disasters.

Risk analysis: The process of analyzing threats and vulnerabilities.

Root cause: The primary underlying reason or cause behind an effect.

Root cause analysis: An in-depth process for identifying and correcting the fundamental factor beneath any variation in performance. Technique used to find the underlying cause of a problem.

Run chart: Line graph of key data plotted over time.

Scorecard: A tool to visualize measurements of key performance indicators for an organization relative to time, targets, or other baselines. Also, sometimes referred to as dashboards.

Sigma: Mathematical term for standard deviation, annotated by the Greek letter σ.

Simulation: A logical or mathematical model of a process or system. Computer-based modeling technique used as an abstract representation of a real system.

Six Sigma: Methodology focused on improving processes and quality by eliminating defects and reducing variability or volatility of outcomes.

Skewness: Asymmetry of the data.

Stakeholder: Internal and external interested parties in an organization and its initiative.

Standard deviation: The primary statistical measure of variability or dispersion in data observations.

Statistical process control: A term used for applying statistics to monitor and control the behavior of a process.

Strategy: Direction and choice of a unique and valuable position rooted in systems of activities that are difficult to match.

Structured Query Language (SQL): A programming tool used to gather data from an application database.

Surge capacity: The ability to rapidly expand services to meet increased demand, especially during times of disaster.

Swim lane: A depiction of the boundaries between processes and the cross-functionality between various parties to execute a business process.

Systems orientation: The notion that all activities and processes are interconnected, and that change in one area produces change elsewhere.

Table: An element of a computer database made up of rows and columns.

Target: A performance value that an organization is trying to achieve through a plan or project.

Telehealth: The use of audio and visual technology to deliver care and other services.

Theory of constraints: A quality improvement method that addresses the effect of system constraints on performance outcomes.

Throughput: The rate or velocity at which services are performed or goods are delivered. Refers to the amount of outputs that a process can deliver over a specific time period, and is used in both productivity analysis and process engineering.

Time: Key parameter using in process modeling, defined as the differential between the time an activity started and ended.

Time and motion study: Analysis of the details of a process, to identify the total amount of time and effort required to perform a procedure.

To-be process: A version of a process map that depicts the future state, or after design and process engineering.

Transparency: An attribute of being clear, so that things can be seen distinctly.

Uncertainty: The lack of knowing what the future will hold: The quantification of uncertainty is by incorporating risk into models:

Unstructured data: Data compiled in a computer system that are not readily amenable to statistical analysis, such as an x-ray image or an electrocardiogram (EKG) tracing.

Validation: The term used in modeling to describe the act of ensuring that the model reflects reality.

Value: An expression of the relationship between outcomes produced by an organization and costs over time.

Value-based financing: An alternative to fee for service, focused on paying providers based on the value and quality of services provided.

Value stream mapping: A technique where all tasks and action in a process are modeled visually to show all activities performed from start to finish. Used in Lean methodologies.

Variability: The relative degree of dispersion of data points, especially as they differ from the norm. Inconsistency of results. Variability in process outcomes is the major source of operational inefficiency, and should be minimized as much as possible. Measured by standard deviation or coefficient of variation.

Variable: A column in a table within a database.

Wait time: Time interval during which there is a temporary cessation of service.

Work breakdown structure (WBS): Breaking a project up into specific tasks and functions by responsible party.

Zero defects: Philosophy that expects managers to prevent errors before they begin, reducing total costs and doing things right the first time.

Index

Printed in the United States
by Baker & Taylor Publisher Services